$1—

Be Your Own Politician

Be Your Own Politician

Why It's Time for a New Kind of Politics

Paul Twivy

Biteback Publishing

First published in Great Britain in 2015 by
Biteback Publishing Ltd
Westminster Tower
3 Albert Embankment
London SE1 7SP

ISBN 978-1-84954-886-1

10 9 8 7 6 5 4 3 2 1

A CIP catalogue record for this book is available from the British Library.

Set in Adobe Garamond Pro

Printed and bound in Great Britain by
CPI Group (UK) Ltd, Croydon CR0 4YY

To my children, Sam, Josh, Max, Eve and Clara, because, in five entirely unique ways, they make me optimistic about the future.

With thanks to my parents, Sam and Sheila Twivy, for their love, energy, humour and values; my wife, Gaby Guz, for her loving companionship and forensic honesty; to David Robinson for constant inspiration; to Camila Batmanghelidjh, Tom Calderbank, Richard Edwards, Neil Jameson, Bill Lawns, Sam Massey, Jane Tewson, Derek and Doug Williams and countless other everyday heroes without whom their communities, and our society, would collapse; to my Your Square Mile team, especially Jamie Cowen, Andrew Dick, Emma Howard, Ollie Levy, June Mason, Olivier Severs, Timothy Rice and Emily Wilkie; to Tony Morris and Peter Collett for their help with this book.

Contents

PART TWO:
A NEW KIND OF POLITICS AND
A STRONGER SOCIETY

Never doubt that a small group of thoughtful, committed citizens can change the world. Indeed, it is the only thing that ever has.

— Margaret Mead, cultural anthropologist

Long-term sustainable change happens if people discover their own power. The key is moving the centre of gravity in the decision-making, move it closer to people in the community and away from a centrally directed, top-down approach. For the first time in human history, technology is enabling people to really maintain those rich connections with much larger numbers of people than ever before.

— Pierre Omidyar, founder of eBay

Be the change that you want to see in the world.

— Mahatma Gandhi, father of the Indian nation

She would rather light candles than curse the darkness.

— Adlai Stevenson on Eleanor Roosevelt, the longest-serving First Lady of America, who oversaw the drafting of the Universal Declaration of Human Rights

Paul Twivy photographed by *The Times* commenting on the UK riots in 2011.

Introduction: Why it's time for a new kind of politics, business and volunteering

W HEN YOU STAND BACK and draw breath, there is little real democracy in the United Kingdom, despite a long and vibrant democratic tradition. The 'mother of all parliaments' is neglecting her children.

The theory is that the UK Parliament is the coming together

of 650 MPs representing, on average, almost 100,000 constituents each. Issues and solutions should therefore be able to rise bottom-up as well as top-down.

The reality is that MPs aren't representative: only twenty-seven MPs are from ethnic minority backgrounds and only 147 are women. Many are career politicians with little experience of the working-day world about which they make decisions.

Political strategy for the 2015 general election seems to already be focusing on fourteen marginal seats and as few as 220,000 swing voters who might determine the outcome of a complex, four- or five-party contest.

The major political parties reduce the ability of MPs to genuinely represent the views of their local constituents, with the whip system forcing them to toe the line on so many issues. No longer is Parliament an aggregate of local needs debated at national level.

Most people in the UK feel most of the time as if they are watching the spectacle of a small body of powerful people or organisations make the real decisions behind closed doors. They have lost the knowledge of how to influence and the habit of trying. They need to re-develop a sense of how their individual actions make a difference.

Voting once every five years is not the same as democracy. 'Interactive, responsive government' is an aspiration cherished by many, promised by a number of political leaders, including our last three prime ministers, but definitely not yet a reality.

In 2010/11, according to the Citizenship Survey by the Department for Communities and Local Government

(DCLG), fewer than four in ten people – 38 per cent – felt they could influence decisions in their local area, despite three-quarters of them – 74 per cent – saying it was important. Forty-four per cent want to be more involved in decisions made by their council.

Only one in three people – 34 per cent – participated in civic life in the last twelve months. Participation includes simply contacting an elected representative such as a councillor or MP; two-thirds of people had no contact.[1]

Only 3 per cent of people attend public meetings, although this tells you as much about how they are conducted and publicised as much as anything else.

So there is a widespread thirst for participation in democracy – and it isn't being quenched.

Thinking about the other end of the telescope, many have talked about the lack of real power even at the centre of political life. Rory Stewart has said that being an MP is the most powerless position he has ever held and wrote memorably:

> This is the age of *The Wizard of Oz*, you know. In the end you get behind the curtain and you finally meet the wizard – and there's this tiny, frightened figure. I think

---

[1]   As an interesting footnote, Eric Pickles, supposedly one of the champions of the Big Society, cancelled the citizenship survey from which these facts derive. This was supposedly because it was complex – so complex that it had already run very smoothly for ten years! Perhaps Mr Pickles was worried about what it might show in relation to the Big Society's effects, or lack thereof, which it was perfectly equipped to measure.

every prime minister has sort of said this since Blair. You
get there and you pull the lever, and nothing happens.

So this system is not working for anyone: neither the tiny
minority apparently in power nor the powerless majority. It's
time to tear down the Berlin Wall between politicians and
citizens and reconnect. The United Kingdom invented modern parliamentary democracy. We now need to reinvent it.

The Tories created the rhetoric of the Big Society without delivering on the substance or enabling mechanisms.
It sounded very welcome, for example, that a petition with
100,000 signatures could trigger a parliamentary debate. In
reality, these debates are usually staged on a Friday when most
MPs are in their constituencies.

Participatory budgeting doesn't happen nearly enough,
and when it does it's often confined to a single area of spending, such as childcare. The demands on councils to publish
all their spending has often simply resulted in laundry lists
that even the most time-rich and determined citizen activist
would struggle to build into a coherent picture of priorities.

In an age where people can interrogate most companies
and products online as well as elsewhere, government still
remains largely remote and inscrutable. We need to create
new links between individuals and government.

This is akin to retraining the neural pathways or muscles
in a damaged human body so that the brain can once again
move the hands.

We need to consciously map out the concentric circles

of influence that spread outwards from the epicentre of our personal lives and flow inwards from the global effects of climate change, limited resources, international trade, so that we know how we can participate and influence again.

We now face the most unsatisfactory general election imaginable. UKIP is growing in popularity and has won its first parliamentary seat. Its potency is in saying no to political correctness 'because it stifles free speech' – epitomised by Nigel Farage, the man with the blunt opinions and a pint of beer surgically attached to one hand.

In an age that still adheres to Blair and Campbell's inheritance of strict political whipping and sophisticated media training, never has nothing been said by so many politicians at such great length. So brevity and clarity and down-to-earth language such as UKIP's shine, but how deceptively.

UKIP has some positive things to say, such as: 'Teach children positive messages and pride in their country.' They have some potentially sensible individual policies, such as the creation of new grammar schools, which could increase social mobility if handled properly, and locally elected county health boards to inspect hospitals. They also support regular, Swiss-style referenda that involve the public in key issues and open the window to the fresh air of public opinion in the stuffy, cloistered world of Parliament (and yes, I do realise that MPs hold surgeries with their constituents and visit factories and hospitals!) However, look at the hatred lurking within UKIP…

Look at the ignorance of wanting to scrap all green taxes;

the reactionary nimbyism of scrapping wind turbine subsidies because they are popularly viewed as an eyesore, doubtless from the pub window; yet the confident assertion that shale gas is perfectly fine.

UKIP preach for British workers to be given first crack at jobs that we all know many British workers already rejected and which we have all relied on immigrants to do. Worst of all is their desire to cut foreign aid, one of the defining things that stop this small island becoming just that. Of course it must be rigorously checked that it doesn't get wasted or misdirected, but let's be realistic: UKIP is the face of xenophobia and protectionism.

Hang your heads in shame, Mr Farage & co., when you ask that immigrants must financially support themselves for five years with private education, private housing and private healthcare, with access to the UK denied unless there is evidence of private health insurance.

This is to deny the NHS (except, graciously, in emergencies) to immigrants, who form a large proportion of its staff. Is this what UKIP would have done to the waves of needy immigrants who have been welcomed to these shores and, as in the USA, have considerably enriched its culture and economic wealth?

> Give me your tired, your poor,
> Your huddled masses yearning to breathe free,
> The wretched refuse of your teeming shore.
> Send these, the homeless, tempest-tossed, to me:

I lift my lamp beside the golden door.
– *Emma Lazarus, as inscribed on the Statue of Liberty in New York*

Dare send me your tired, your poor,
Your huddled masses yearning to rape our state,
The wretched refuse of your teeming shore,
Keep out, the homeless, EU-tossed to Britain Great.
I lift my pint beside the old saloon door.
– *Nigel Farage (imagined)*

Can Cameron, the great centre-right reformer, be seriously considering an electoral pact with UKIP? His uncosted tax cuts to the middle class whilst freezing the benefits of 8.5 million people who are poor certainly looks like pragmatism to win a majority of the right-leaning at all costs. It also looks foolish, as the deficit, despite good early progress, has not been cut at all this year.

How sad is it that Ed Miliband, sincere and brave though he has been in many fights he has taken on and individual policies he has promoted, should be retreating to a safe Old Labour heartland, hoping that the maths of smaller Labour constituencies will win him enough seats to scrape in or to form a coalition if needed?

The truth is that as left and right separate more and more, and the Liberal Democrats implode and simply hope to stay in power by holding its balance, politics needs to move beyond tribal loyalties.

Left and right are not the issue any more, just as Green should no longer be a party but rather a universal strategy. We need to re-dimensionalise and reinvent politics altogether.

If nothing else, irrefutable maths requires this. The irrefutable maths that we have a maximum of forty years to save the planet, the next ten being the most critical. The irrefutable maths that we need to actively engage the NHS staff and the public to resolve the funding gap for the NHS by being proactively involved in everything from better diets and more exercise to improve health; to constant improvement of care by pooling the observations and ideas of front-line staff; to deciding whether we charge for specific services or circumstances. Thirty per cent of people who turn up to A&E are there because of alcohol, for example. Should they be challenged to change their behaviour or face being charged or, at least, put at the back of the queue?

The irrefutable maths is that we have only reduced the budget deficit from a peak of £162.7 billion in 2009/10 to £102.3 billion in 2013/14, despite the promise by George Osborne to reduce it to £37 billion by 2015, thereby, in his mind, balancing the enormous books on sturdy Tory knees. In fact, the deficit is likely to be cut by only a further £5 billion in 2014/15 to a predicted £97 billion. Our cumulative government debt has risen now to the point where it is almost £24,000 per person, or £57,000 per household. That is our collective, national debt expressed in personal terms.

The numbers reflect not just the economic facts but also the lack of a powerful ideology to inspire people, to bind us as citizens into a common purpose. No politicians try to raise our individual or national self-esteem. No politicians invite us to improve the delivery of services in the profession or sector in which we work, or give us the tools by which to achieve it. Yet the technology to enable all of us to be involved has never been more plentiful.

If you want to improve the traffic flow and road safety in any UK city, why not give 500 taxi drivers, bus drivers, cyclists and home delivery drivers the means of recording ideas, taking photos, feeding in live data via devices in their vehicles and a dedicated website? Why not balance this with the views of 500 able-bodied and disabled pedestrians/users of public transport? The same principle applies to all services and aspects of our public life.

Income tax revenue this year has barely increased since the previous year, despite one million more people being in employment and unemployment falling to its lowest level since 2008, because so much of that employment is low-paid work on zero-hour contracts.

This means that *all* businesses need to pay their proper taxes. It means all tax loopholes for the wealthy need to be shut. It means re-banding council tax even if it is complicated and labour-intensive to set up. It means businesses need to do much more than just pay lip-service via corporate social responsibility: they need to act as societies themselves and see their societal and commercial purpose as a unified whole.

It also means that we need to start supporting social entrepreneurs more, seeing charities and social enterprises as intellectual property owners and cost-effective solvers of social problems as well as humane, not-for-profit organisations.

Finally, it means a radical reinvention of action-oriented politics.

Scotland has just rejected independence and re-embraced the union of the United Kingdom on new, more devolved terms promised solemnly by the three main UK party leaders, by a vote of 55 per cent to 45 per cent. The turnout, at almost 85 per cent, was the highest in any UK election since 1951 and demonstrates that when crucial issues that eclipse party politics and relate to fundamental identity and collective ambition are put to the vote, the electricity of true democracy returns.

It has been compelling and uplifting to see the passion, the soul- and fact-searching and the high and intelligent standard of debate. It was particularly moving to see many sixteen- and seventeen-year-olds asking incisive questions: reasons to be optimistic for years to come.

As we discovered in a much more modest way in our Your Square Mile communities across the UK, the importance and power of well-run public meetings and debates cannot be underestimated, and the Scottish referendum proved this. Issues become real when they come attached to people. Face-to-face assemblies are still the truest form of 'social media' for spreading, hearing and strengthening new ideas.

People in Scotland, as elsewhere, are utterly fed up with so many decisions being made remotely in Westminster. At an even more local level, the Scottish islands still feel that

Edinburgh is pretty remote as well, even if it is preferable to Westminster.

In other words, people are starting to declare very passionately the level at which they feel they can genuinely have a say and need to have an influence. It seems to have strong echoes of what the ancient Greeks felt about cradling democracy in Athens: that once you get beyond 15,000 to 20,000 people – the *polis* or city from which the name 'politics' is derived – it's difficult for people to really feel they have influence.

We need many more mayors leading cities; much more participatory budgeting by local authorities; a north of England and a Midlands Assembly; citizens' juries and regular votes and informed debates, both digitally and in public meetings, on issues as critical as immigration, food poverty, the housing crisis, care for the elderly and the future of the NHS. That way we can live up to what the Athenians created and held dear: true democracy.

This book is about how each and every one of us can change the UK. It is built on a rephrasing of John F. Kennedy: 'Ask both what your country can do for you and what you can do for your country.' The world thrives on mutual self-interest rather than pure selflessness. It is in the mutual self-interest of the state and the citizen to form a new relationship of collaboration.

The Occupy movement has drawn much attention to vital, democratic causes and inequalities in London, New York, Hong Kong and elsewhere. I am interested in the 64.1 million of us who do occupy the UK in becoming Occupy UK: a collective movement to improve our lives and society for all. This might be naïve and ambitious, but how do we ever progress without naïve, ambitious ideas?

Part One of this book is my experience of how to successfully conduct public campaigns and start social movements. This draws on my experience as an advisor to Comic Relief for twenty-five years; as one of the founders of TimeBank; as the editor and collator of *Change the World for a Fiver*; as the co-founder of The Big Lunch with Tim Smit; as the founder of Your Square Mile; and as the one-time CEO of the ill-fated but instructive Big Society Network.

I have visited 10 Downing Street some thirty-five to forty times over three decades, but I have picked out ten visits that have been significant and revealing: *Ten to Ten*. I have tried to describe the centre of power in this country from the point of view of someone who has never run for, or held, political office.

My journey behind the shiny, terrorist-proof, steel black door with the distinctive squashed oval 'o' in '10' stretches from tackling Margaret Thatcher on the NHS, to working extensively with Gordon Brown on tackling tough societal issues, to being asked by David Cameron to help lead the Big Society.

I have told the unvarnished and often complex truth, and part of this truth is that if I can fight for causes with prime ministers and sometimes win, anyone can. I have had the privilege of an excellent education, but I do not come from a particularly privileged or influential background.

My father was from a working-class part of Leeds and became a GP in the NHS, working hard and dedicating himself to the public for forty years, refusing to ever have private patients. His father, in turn, was an accountant who worked all hours to balance the books of a modest firm, and his mother was a piano teacher.

My mother came from a large, loving family in Essex and she trained as a nurse, raised my sisters and me, gave Red Cross classes and helped run the NSPCC, eventually at county level. Her mother was Irish and sadly died young and her father was a successful surveyor and engineer.

My parents gave me love and values but not privilege. They were both dedicated to public service. My parents voted Tory because they were royalist, patriotic, believed in hard work and thrift and associated the Conservatives with their beloved Church of England. Their politics were a set of visceral reactions, a culture.

This had a powerful effect on me and has made my political journey unusual. The stereotype is that if you're not left-wing when you're young you've got no heart and if you're not right-wing when you're older you've got no sense. This statement is uniquely ageist in two different directions. I have progressively moved further left the older I've got, but my main interest is going beyond left and right to a new, modern kind of democracy.

I have experienced a lot of success but also much failure in my professional life. I have often had to rely on stamina, a degree of cunning and sheer bloody-mindedness to get things

PAUL TWIVY

done. I have met people from far tougher backgrounds than mine who have achieved far greater things and in some of the poorest neighbourhoods in the UK. They are the real heroes. They have tackled problems which threatened to engulf them, against the odds. I have told a few of their stories, which I hope will inspire you to make change in your neighbourhood, city or even country.

In Part One, I also want to show how, after the harsh economics of Thatcher, there has been a golden thread of ideology, of good intents, running from Blair through Brown to Cameron. This thread – stretching from Blair's 'Giving Age' through Brown's 'Council on Social Action' to Cameron's 'Big Society' – has been about a new kind of relationship between citizens and politics. Yet the dream has never quite become a reality.

In Part Two, I describe how a better UK can come to fruition but how politics needs to change for that to happen; how we need to transform our outdated views on charities and social entrepreneurs; how businesses need to go well beyond the platitudes of corporate social responsibility, becoming societies in and of themselves that contribute to society, as did their Victorian forerunners. They will paradoxically become more commercially successful in the process. I have also suggested an idea for a People's Parliament, parallel to Parliament itself, in which we vote for 650 of the UK's best problem-solvers who match and shadow our 650 MPs.

If that all sounds a little heavy, then fear not, for there are jokes, gossip, anecdotes, scandals and colourful characters in abundance. Why would one want to do anything unless there is a large dollop of fun involved?

PART ONE

TEN TO TEN – THE POLITICS OF GOOD INTENTIONS

Chapter 1

The nature of Downing Street

ACROSS THREE DECADES I have visited 10 Downing Street some thirty to forty times, all of them memorable and different, a few of them publicised and significant, many private and revealing. I have seen it from the various perspectives of dinner guest, advisor, commentator, researcher, social entrepreneur, committee member, personal friend and citizen. I have also never quite lost two prisms: that of the privileged observer and the social reformer. All of my visits have been about tackling social problems.

During a few periods of frequent, close-together visits, Downing Street has become almost familiar: like a workplace. Yet I have never become blasé about its astonishing significance, or stopped being wary about the distorting and giddying vortex it creates as a centre of power, changing people's behaviour, including my own.

I have seen the house – for that indeed, in prosaic terms, is what it is – in many moods. I have sat in what used to be Margaret Thatcher's study on a quiet Friday afternoon, with the house largely deserted, and the light fading across St James's Park, with a friend who was working inside No. 10.

I have had a fascinating three-hour chat about the nature of society with a Prime Minister's closest advisor, having had a blazing row with him the day before just behind the famous front door.

I have found myself, for a few minutes, alone with Gordon Brown beaming with pride at his young son in a quiet, intimate moment on the No. 11 staircase.

I have sat around the Cabinet table with David Cameron, Nick Clegg and twenty of the most inspiring social entrepreneurs in the UK, in the first meeting to be held after the first Cabinet meeting of the new coalition, on a brilliant, sunlit day bathed in optimism and the energy of new power.

What has fascinated me is the sheer complexity and oddity of what I have witnessed. I have seen John Major, stereotyped as a decent but essentially grey man, be colourful, satirical and brimming over with anecdotes. I have witnessed the diamond-like political brilliance but also the deep insecurity and self-consciousness of Tony Blair.

My encounters with Gordon Brown revealed a diverse blend of passionate social reformer, doting dad, awkward non-delegator and angry obsessive, a man with soul, to my mind often misunderstood. David Cameron I found to be oozing with self-assured wit and charm but also quite vulnerable, permeable and a potentially powerful social reformer in the right circumstances.

These individual human beings, who have risen by willpower, ambition, nous, diplomacy, nerve and tenacity to the highest position in the land, are multifaceted, despite our desire to put them in a simple straitjacket of a certain ideology, a caricatured personality type or a set of achievements.

When you see them at work, at the centre of the spider's web of political influence, their human frailty and occasional ordinariness makes the role of Prime Minister seem both more within reach and more extraordinary and remarkable in equal measure. As I mentioned in my introduction, Rory Stewart talked recently of *The Wizard of Oz* effect of pulling back the curtain in politics, even the centre of politics, to find that no one really has any power.

I remember hearing one of the chancellors describing what it is like to raise or lower interest rates in order to produce a macro-economic effect. He described it as like having the most enormous garden hose imaginable. You switch on the tap a little and run down to the other end to see if any water is coming out. Nothing emerges. You go back to the tap and increase the flow of water. You run back to the end of the hose to find an inadequate dribble. Exasperated, you turn the tap on full, run to the end of the hose, peer into its darkness – and a flood of water blows your head off.

Such is the crudity of pushing interest rates – higher or lower – through a whole economic system that involves the arteries and veins of intermediaries, banks, businesses and millions of individual lending, borrowing and investing decisions. It's like over-steering a super-tanker and having to constantly correct in anticipation of the coming miles.

To me, this story is a paradigm of the whole power of No. 10 and Parliament. It is crude and top-down and subject to the massive complexity of human motivation and mood. Ultimately, all politics are local, and national politics are often an aggregate of local politics. There is both enormous power in the roles of Prime Minister and Cabinet, and an enormous lack of power in their disconnect from how things play out every day and how daily events affect the national mood and motivation.

In this sense, it is wholly appropriate that No. 10 is just a Georgian terraced house in the centre of London, although even that status places it way above many homes in the land.

When I gave a speech at Downing Street with David Cameron early on in his premiership, he said to the guests, with all the self-knowing charm of how to flatter and simultaneously be self-deprecating, 'Welcome to my modest, new, Georgian home.'

No. 10 doesn't have the conscious grandeur of many presidential homes and palaces except in a few of its larger entertaining rooms. Yet despite playing host to lots of charity and 'thank you to ordinary citizens' events, it is in perennial and increasing danger of being an untouchable fortress.

It is always worth looking behind familiar facades, walking round the back of the film set, and there is no more fascinating façade and film set than 10 Downing Street.

What became Westminster started life as Thorney Island. Before it became this vital island of power within the larger island of Great Britain, it started in an unprepossessing way as a marshy piece of land lying between two branches of the river Tyburn, which flowed from Hampstead Heath to the Thames. It was chosen by the Romans as a site for early settlement and was also beset with plague.

King Canute later built a palace there and Edward the Confessor and William the Conqueror maintained a royal presence. It became a significant centre of power after Westminster Abbey was constructed. Royalty first dignified Westminster, the Church then sanctified it and political power finally seized it.

It's rather wonderful that the first domestic building on what is now Downing Street was the Axe Brewery, which became dilapidated and collapsed in the 1500s. This irreverent and bohemian predecessor to the home of prime ministers brings it nicely down to earth.

The building of Whitehall Palace by Henry VIII cemented Westminster's position as the centre of power and Downing

Street stands on the edge of what was the palace site before it was destroyed by fire in 1698.

Sir Thomas Knyvett, an MP and a Justice of the Peace famous for arresting Guy Fawkes, built the first domestic house in Downing Street, which then passed to his descendants, including the aunt of Oliver Cromwell.

However, the most amusing aspect of Downing Street's history belongs to its namesake. George Downing was something of a rogue. A former diplomat at The Hague serving the Commonwealth, he frequently changed allegiance with aplomb. He traded enough secrets to gain a royal pardon in March 1660.

Interested in power and money, he saw an opportunity to make his fortune in property. In 1682, he secured the leases for Downing Street and commissioned Sir Christopher Wren to design new houses. So far, so good!

In order to maximise profit, however, the houses were cheaply built, with poor foundations for the boggy ground. Sir Winston Churchill later complained that the houses on Downing Street were 'shaky and lightly built by the profiteering contractor whose name they bear'.

It fell, paradoxically, to Tony Blair to invest in the refurbishing of Downing Street to make it structurally sound: to some people's minds, the shakiest Prime Minister. Perhaps this is one of his soundest achievements for posterity!

A somewhat grander house, owned by the daughter of Charles II, with a wonderful view over Horse Guards, was back to back with the 'the Johnny-come-lately' terraced houses of Downing Street. She complained bitterly.

When George II gave the house to Sir Robert Walpole, effectively the first Prime Minister, he conjoined it with the grander house behind. This explains why Downing Street is effectively a TARDIS. You enter one of a number of terraced houses, now all interconnected and, as you walk through to the back, you enter a much grander house that now provides all the entertainment rooms.

The effect is extraordinary. The frontage is smart Georgian but very modest compared to, say, the White House. Yet it gives way to grandeur. This feels somehow symbolic of some aspects of the British character: speak softly but carry a big stick.

The lion's head knocker on the front door reinforces this sense, as does the title 'First Lord of the Treasury' engraved on the brass letterbox: rather than prosaically stating 'Residence of the Prime Minister', one has to ask the historical meaning of the more lateral title given originally to Walpole. The title is, if you think about it, a rather regal rendition of 'Chief Accountant'.

Many eighteenth- and nineteenth-century prime ministers chose not to live in Downing Street but simply used it as their office, and by 1830 there were plans to tear it down because the surrounding area had become so seedy. Disraeli and Gladstone restored it to its former glory and the rest, as they say, is history.

When I was a child, and Heath and Wilson were prime ministers, I used to go with my mum to Downing Street. You could stroll down the street free from any barriers or police checks and stand outside waiting for famous people to enter or leave. If you were as charming as my mum, you could even get the policeman on duty to take your picture in front of the famous front door.

Now the impregnable gates stand guard at the end of the street. You have to go through an initial check of your name on a list and the up-and-down-glance scrutiny of photo ID; then go through the side gate and airport-style scanning in a sentry hut.

Whilst the difficulty of gaining access is understandable, post-terrorist attacks and in a modern world when the greatest enemy might be a single individual with a monstrous cause, it doesn't help to so dramatically separate power from those affected by it.

Downing Street, as a street, feels like being on a film set because of its over-familiarity on the one hand but also because of it being an ordinary if rather spacious road, but brutally stripped of cars, prams, bikes (apart from Andrew Mitchell's), screaming children, recycling boxes and all the other paraphernalia of street life. It's slightly eerie; an isolation chamber or open-air vault separating the public scrambling at the gate from the scurrying figures of power inside the house. It's like walking into your own *Truman Show*.

When they are present, cameras, multiple or singular, add to this sense of Downing Street as a theatre. Yet even when cameras are not present, it feels as if they are. This theatre has seen the sorry farce of downfall as Cabinet ministers and even prime ministers are exiled from power and the soaring triumph of a freshly elected PM or a presidential visit.

The faint resonance of these mixed emotions pervades the often-empty street: the tearful but proud final drive to Parliament for Margaret Thatcher; the helicopter-viewed grand entrance of Tony Blair; the final, defiantly personal walk of Gordon and Sarah Brown with their two children, hidden from cameras before and since, stripped of power but not of parenthood.

The famous door is interesting in and of itself. There is no key, not even for the Prime Minister. It cannot be opened from the outside. There is always someone to open it from the inside. Sometimes this happens without you knocking, either by the happy accident of someone departing at the same time or by being viewed approaching the door on a camera. This swinging open of the door at your presence adds a fairytale 'Open Sesame' kind of charm. At other times you have to knock, which makes one feel like a potentially unworthy intruder.

As a friend of mine, the behavioural psychologist Peter Collett, astutely observed, the steps of No. 10 have witnessed some of the best examples of 'doorstepping', whereby one leader tries to demonstrate superiority over the other by allowing them through a door first, even pushing them.

This appears to treat the other person as superior but is actually saying, 'I have the magnanimity and status to let you go first.' President Mitterrand was a master of 'doorstepping', attempting it with British PMs even on their own threshold.

One can usually just glimpse the entrance vestibule of No. 10 on television as prime ministers and Cabinet ministers emerge to wave, speak, deal with a re-shuffle or simply leave for Parliament in a rush of button-tightening of their jackets, carrying briefing documents, surrounded by sideways- and upwards-glancing security men.

It is an ample size but not overwhelming: beautifully proportioned to allow the smooth flow of many people at once, as if on a film set. It contains a small number of beautiful objects all ranged around the walls: a grandfather clock, paintings and the famous hooded Chippendale 'Guard's Chair'.

This accentuates the space in the middle, which is dominated by the black and white chequered floor: an appropriate chessboard to warm up the tactics of all visiting politicians and dignitaries before they ply their arguments in the Cabinet Room. It is similar to the entrance hall of Claridge's but less highly polished.

Somehow, there is a fairytale-like quality to the hall. It feels like a scene in *Alice in Wonderland*. The White Rabbit might fall down the chimney at any moment and scurry off to an important meeting, almost bowling you over. You are Alice, suddenly feeling smaller compared to the significance of your surroundings.

When you gaze at the space behind the door – possibly the most famous off-stage place on earth – you can't help thinking of Thatcher, in tears, supported by Denis as she left for Parliament on her last day as PM, perhaps steadied by a loyal doorman. Or Churchill pacing out, puffed up with sturdy resolve, another brilliant speech being hammered out on the anvil of his brain.

From the entrance hall, you can go left to wait in a few small areas with stairs rising above you – there appear to be a myriad of staircases like an Escher drawing – or you can proceed straight ahead down a corridor that leads to the Cabinet Room. From here you can turn right up the Grand Staircase, passing the famous array of drawings and photographs of every Prime Minister in chronological order.

Upstairs, you enter the Terracotta Room and Pillared Room, often open together to host receptions whose treasures include a famous portrait of Elizabeth I, and William Pitt the Younger's desk.

As I have increased my familiarity with the seat of power, so I have also considerably increased my experience of the toughest and poorest communities in the UK. This has led me to 'mind the gap' and has led to my view that modern politics needs to change; it needs to become more devolved, more genuinely democratic, more of a balance between local-up and national-down. It needs to dramatically increase its use of digital, interactive technologies.

As prime ministers move from the initial tourist pleasure and astonishment at the surroundings of history in which they too can create history, and become enmeshed in sofa coteries of advisors, the perspectives on ordinary people on the challenges of everyday life shorten as the sun of power rises to midday. Perhaps this is inevitable. Perhaps it provides a useful distance from clamouring voices and a multitude of individual needs. Perhaps there needs to be a different way, as I will explore in this book.

One of the first generation of NHS general managers, as portrayed
in an advertising campaign by the Royal College of Nursing.

Chapter 2

Tackling Thatcher on health

I JOINTLY LED FOUR CAMPAIGNS involving Margaret Thatcher as Prime Minister. They were all related to health. One was about litter, commissioned by her and soon abandoned by her. The second was fighting her on the Griffiths reorganisation of the NHS, which introduced general managers for the first time and removed matrons. The third was to lobby her and Nigel Lawson to abolish the tobacco sponsorship of sport. Finally, I was part of a campaign to try to change sexual behaviour as the Aids crisis hit and the government resorted to doom-mongering as a public awareness strategy. These provided my earliest perspectives on politics and how it does – or doesn't – respond to societal need.

In the mid-1980s, I was a partner in an ad agency with the Pythonesque name of 'Still Price Court Twivy D'Souza'. It was the longest and silliest name in advertising. At the end of our first year we ran an ad featuring all the mis-spelt envelopes we had received, including 'Swill Trice Coup Privy and de Croupier'!

We won the account for a fledgling airline with one plane, called Virgin Atlantic. I hand-delivered a cheeky but well-researched letter to Richard Branson on the houseboat that had been his home and was now his office on the canal in Little Venice. The letter pointed out that his airline was great but its advertising wasn't and that there was a unique opportunity to cut through the hyperbole of his rivals' campaigns.

He phoned up immediately and told me I was a 'cheeky sod' but that if we could, within twenty-four hours, create a witty ad to promote his Atlantic Cup Challenge – to cross the said ocean in record time – we could have the airline account. We did it and we won the account.

Thus started a partnership and friendship with Richard that has lasted to this day. When he won the Atlantic Cup, Mrs Thatcher climbed aboard his speedboat as he took a victory trip up the Thames. Thatcher was never one to miss a glamorous PR shoot or an opportunity to claim British heroes. She was also a terrible flirt!

A few weeks later, the PM asked Richard to help solve Britain's chronic litter problems. The term 'tsar' hadn't yet been contorted into meaning 'someone in charge of an almost impossible public need that the government of the day wishes to delegate, put at arm's length or blame on someone else', as in 'drugs tsar'. Branson's appointment by Mrs T. to clean up Britain was, however, a forerunner of such posts.

Dubbed 'King of Litter' by the tabloids, Richard phoned me up in a panic. What could he do? We did lots of research, which showed that countries such as France, Germany and Japan spent far more per head on clearing litter than the UK. This case for more investment went down very badly with the PM, of course.

We also suggested lots of inventive 'market economy' ideas we felt she would like, such as commercially sponsored litter bins; dustcarts carrying paid-for advertising as they drove through the streets; dustmen being officially allowed to take second jobs; tougher on-the-spot-fines for dropping chewing gum, which costs hundreds of millions of pounds a year to scrape off the pavements.

Even these seemingly Thatcherite ideas went nowhere, killed off by the civil service. I have never known any group of people able to absorb, dilute and destroy good ideas as slowly and professionally as civil servants. Nothing is ever rejected per se. It is all absorbed into a grey sea of possibilities, which every five years get washed up on the shore yet again and re-scrutinised like fascinating flotsam. This is not to say that the civil service don't achieve some excellent things.

The value of their continuity is made clear when you look at the US, where all the public servants as well as the politicians change in a new administration.

Anyway, as an advertising agency, we cut our teeth on fast-moving, apparently impenetrable problems. With this strong reputation came some very interesting approaches, but none more interesting or important than from the Royal College of Nursing.

The Royal College of Nursing, or RCN for short, was led at that time by the remarkable and charismatic Trevor Clay. Trevor had been one of the first male nurses in the UK, but that was just the start of his remarkable career. During his time as general secretary at the RCN, from 1982 to 1989, it became the fastest-growing trade union and the largest outside the Trades Union Congress. By the time he retired, it had over 285,000 members. This was despite Trevor suffering from severe emphysema since the age of thirty-seven.

Trevor and a few trusted members of his team arrived in our office one afternoon. In a passionate speech, at times almost incoherent with disbelief and rage, he outlined how the reorganisation of the health service, following the Griffiths Report on care in the community, was rapidly destroying the role of nurses and threatening the fundamentals of patient care. The report had been commissioned by Margaret Thatcher in 1984 and led to the introduction of general managers in the health service for the first time.

Mrs Thatcher had decided that nothing was better for the NHS – the 'patient' in her mind – than a large (unmeasured) dose of private sector management.

'Look at these!' Trevor pleaded, splashing a spray of documents in front of us. What lay inside were myriad examples of the stupidity and worse that had followed from the rise to power of business managers unaccustomed to managing health issues and their complexities.

The changes included the almost total demise of the matron – something that had been kept quiet from the public. It occurred to me that perhaps Margaret Thatcher feared other women as capable but more empathetic than her: the matrons who effectively ran large hospitals.

Many have observed that she may have been a female pioneer herself but preferred to surround herself with men rather than women. Margaret had to be the sole femme fatale or 'matron'.

Examples of the appalling decisions made by general managers included two sections of the same hospital, split by a dual carriageway running between them, being forced to share the same emergency defibrillator to save money. In emergencies, if the patient found him or herself in the wrong part of the hospital, the defibrillator had to be rushed across four lanes of traffic, putting medical staff at risk as well as making the patient wait.

People with infectious skin diseases were put on the same wards as geriatrics, susceptible to skin diseases. Mixed wards were created with no dignity or privacy for either gender. Student nurses were left alone at night to supervise wards, sometimes with seriously ill patients. All of this was, of course, to save money.

Whilst the NHS, the biggest employer in Europe then and now, is always in need of efficiency drives, the role of nurses in patient care is incalculable. In addition to their skill, at their best, their ability to care for the entire person transforms the experience and recovery of patients. Matrons and other senior nurses ensured that the front-line knowledge of nurses was at the heart of decision-making, not just the necessarily more clinical and detached views of doctors. All of this was under threat.

Like most British people, I have a deeply ingrained love and respect for the NHS. This is greatly strengthened by the fact that my father was a GP; my mother was a nurse, as were two of my aunts and one of my sisters; and one of my cousins is a distinguished neurosurgeon.

During his time in general practice, my father estimated that he had conducted a million consultations. Not one of them was private. High Court judges and road-sweepers were all treated entirely the same, on a first-come-first-served basis, as they turned up in his surgery. However many people turned up, he didn't leave until everyone had been seen. I also frequently half-woke in the middle of the night to hear Dad going out to visit people who had called in distress in those darkest hours before dawn.

With all that wealth of experience, the only times my father was ever consulted by the Department of Health it was to lecture him about the size of his drugs bill. They asked him to prescribe cheaper, generic versions of drugs. In reply, he pointed out that if patients repeatedly recover from more expensive Antibiotic A in three days, versus five days with less expensive or generic Antibiotic B, then in macro-economic terms, Antibiotic A is cheaper because it gets people back to work as 'economic contributors' faster. This intelligent, front-line experience and feedback is vital and precisely what the RCN was campaigning for the nurses to retain and wield.

We developed a series of hard-hitting black-and-white press ads. One of them carried a headline: 'You're in hospital. It's dark. You're all alone surrounded by strangers. You're worried in case something happens ... and you're the nurse.' Another featured Florence Nightingale on the left and a modern nurse on the right, with the headline: 'The nurse on the left established British nursing standards. The nurse on the right is being forced to compromise them.'

Each ad had an end line succinctly positioning the Royal College of Nursing whilst pointing out its benefit to the general public: 'We care for nurses so they can care for you.'

We made every ad a petition with a simple cut-out-and-post coupon saying, 'I agree that nursing should be run by nurses.'

We ran the ads across a broad range of national press titles in a concentrated burst of energy, supported by PR.

On the first few days after the campaign broke, the RCN had posted one relatively elderly lady in their basement to open and count the petitions as they arrived by mail. Several sacks arrived on the first day and petitions carried on arriving. The elderly lady was rapidly given reinforcements!

In total, the public sent in 250,000 petitions, all signed and identified by name and address. There has, to my knowledge, never been such a huge written response to an ad campaign before or since. Since it only cost £180,000, the value of the campaign was also clear.

In addition to the advertising campaign, we toured the country doing rallies. The speakers were Trevor Clay; Claire Rayner, the well-known agony aunt and former nurse; various politicians, most notably David Owen (memorably described as 'a Prime Minister in search of a party'), who, as a doctor, had some strong opinions on the subject; and myself.

In some venues the audience ran to thousands. I usually spoke last and therefore had plenty of time for the adrenalin to build. I usually started my speech by declaring that my mother was a nurse, as well as my aunts and sister, which led to a cheer of solidarity. This helped to calm my nerves.

As time progressed I got used to the rhythm of connecting with a crowd. On one particular occasion I finished a speech that had got an increasingly warm reception by stating: 'One of our ads points out that most general managers don't know their coccyx from their humerus. I certainly know which of those two parts of the body best suits this government's policy.' I sat down to thunderous applause and Claire Rayner whispered in her breathy, inimitable way, 'Well done, darling!'

I floated on air with the naïve question forming in my mind: 'Is this what it's like to be a politician?' and thinking that I could easily get hooked on the drug. The truth later dawned that rather this was what it's like to be an ideologically driven politician with a self-evidently just cause, and even in those circumstances only on a tiny minority of occasions.

One of the things I found fascinating about David Owen was that he was the only opposition politician who put Thatcher in context. Broadly speaking, he acknowledged her economic achievements and the necessity of some of her reforms but he also saw the many flaws in her social policies. She lacked any kind of broad social empathy (she was apparently often very kind to individuals) in order to achieve her economic reforms, but oh, the damage, much of which has only become truly clear in recent times!

I also learned a couple of other political lessons from Dr Owen. In one conversation he wistfully pointed out to me that it can take a lifetime in politics to get one bill of true significance through Parliament.

On another occasion I was walking with his Parliamentary Private Secretary, who quizzed me about *Spitting Image*. My good friend Ian Hislop was one of the main contributors. In the show, David Steel, the Liberal leader, was always depicted as a tiny puppet in the pocket of the much larger and more powerful David Owen. Owen's PPS asked me the foundation of this stereotype.

I mumbled something about the greater charisma of Owen and then paused. He commented: 'It's interesting because in fact David Steel has the on-the-ground political machinery on which David Owen and the other Social Democrat leaders rely.' Satire, of course, has no interest in these reasoned complexities, but I found it fascinating.

My biggest political education at the time however was with the Royal College of Nursing's political lobbyist, Neil

Stewart. Neil was a tough and canny Scot and a strong and respected union figure as well as lobbyist. He invited me to join him for the House of Commons debate on the reorganisation of the NHS.

He took me to the House of Commons bar before the debate. He then mapped out for me how the debate would run. Scottish Labour would say 'Y' and then the Tories would say 'X'.

'Z', a backbencher, had been planted to throw in a specific spanner in the works. It was intricate, fascinating and he drew it out on a scruffy A4 paper pad with a BIC biro like a battle plan.

In my naïveté, I asked how he could know all of this in advance. He smiled knowingly and we departed for the public gallery. Whilst some details varied and different eddies of argument emerged, the broad flow of the debate, the major positions and manoeuvrings, were as he had described. The chessboard was revealed. I was part shocked and part enthralled. This was a technician describing the engine of realpolitik.

Our campaign built and built. On Valentine's Day in 1987 we delivered 250,000 petitions to Margaret Thatcher at Downing Street with the message 'Put the heart back into the NHS'. I wondered at the time whether the message was too sentimental, but it was clear and emotive.

We succeeded in putting a cogent case to the government of the day and the crucial role of nurses in the re-shaping of the health service was noted and increased, although not as pervasively as one would have hoped. One crucial objective was only achieved much later, when matrons were finally reinstated in 2000 by New Labour. This is a lesson I have had to learn again and again: that campaigns, although they can have significant, short-term impact, can often take a decade or more to achieve true success.

Our agency was consequently, if unofficially, blacklisted for speaking the truth to power, prohibited from pitching for any government advertising until some years later. When finally asked, we blew this opportunity. The brief was to advertise a new benefit payment. At the end of the briefing I said, 'Can I ask a deliberately naïve question? Do you want everyone who is entitled to receive this benefit to be aware of it?'

The silence that followed was ominous, broken only by the most senior civil servant rising up to his full height and saying without a trace of irony, 'Good God, no! The Treasury wouldn't stand for it!'

I cemented my reputation with government by helping Richard Branson and Anita Roddick lobby for the abolition of sports sponsorship by tobacco companies. The association of smoking with sports prowess was obviously damaging, especially to the young.

We suggested that the money lost to sport by banishing this kind of sponsorship could be made up by other, better, sponsors being given a chance and by levying a special tax on every packet of cigarettes to go towards sports education and health campaigns. Nigel Lawson told us that the way the tax system worked, with all tax revenue largely pooled, made this kind of specific allocation of tax near impossible. What was certainly possible was that tobacco company donations and links to the Tory Party were more persuasive than us at this point.

The final health campaign was the most significant. Aids was first officially diagnosed in the US in 1981; first named in 1982; first recognised as a virus in 1983. In 1985, President Bush released billions of dollars to help its prevention and Rock Hudson died of Aids-related illnesses.

The World Health Organization launched its first global Aids programme in 1986. By 1987, Aids activism was underway in many countries and Princess Diana memorably held the hand of an Aids patient to help banish the primitive myth that you shouldn't even touch victims. By then, it was also clear that women, drug users and haemophiliacs as well as gay and bisexual men and women were being infected.

The UK government started a television campaign in 1986. Under a darkened sky, a volcano erupted. Doom-laden images of cascading rocks gave way to shots of a tombstone being chiselled.

John Hurt's magnetic voice gravely intoned: 'There is now a danger that has become a threat to us all. It is a deadly disease and there is no known cure.'

The word etched on to the blackened grave was revealed as 'Aids'. The slogan of the campaign was 'Don't die of ignorance'.

The campaign was very effective in spreading basic awareness, but it also spread panic. It was not as successful at changing sexual habits. This was revealed by many facts, but one in particular was the rise in gonorrhoea and other contact-related sexual diseases. This increase showed that people were not using condoms to anywhere near the degree they claimed in public health research.

A group of us conceived the idea of launching a modern, non-judgemental brand of condoms that was affordable and safe for gay and straight people alike. Importantly, it also had to be pleasurable and appeal to those most at risk and sexually active: the under-25s.

Anita Roddick, Richard Branson, John Jackson and I set about creating and launching Mates condoms. The advertising campaign included six TV commercials across a range of sexual situations. Each of them used the technique from Woody Allen's famous rooftop scene in *Annie Hall* in which subtitles are used to show what the characters are really thinking as opposed to what they are physically saying. We used this technique to empathetically point out that embarrassment and hypocrisy were common issues preventing the use of condoms, but that these had to be confronted.

For the first and only time, we persuaded the BBC to run an unbranded public health version of our films alongside the branded ads on commercial television. This created the so-called roadblock strategy, whereby our ads appeared on every channel simultaneously, exposing them to a large proportion of the nation at once. This was thanks to Michael Grade, who was managing director of the BBC at the time.

When he left the BBC the following year to run Channel 4, one of the reasons he cited for leaving was the stuffy attitude of the governors who eventually forced him to take our films off air on the grounds of 'decency'. It's a classically old-fashioned and damaging attitude: 'Decency before death'. This same attitude leads several people a year to die choking in private rather than 'bother people' to help them. Only in England could politeness cause death.

We also created press ads including one of a sensuous woman staring at the reader, holding a packet of condoms and the line 'They're awfully fiddly to put on. Isn't that half the fun?' Research revealed that by using humour and sex appeal we could get people to change habits who were otherwise untouched by the government's scare-mongering.

Michael Grade, Richard Branson, Alan Maryon Davis and Anita Roddick at the launch of both an Aids awareness campaign and Mates condoms.

The day we launched Mates, we held a press conference at which Michael Grade, Anita Roddick, Richard Branson, our health spokesperson Alan Maryon Davis, John Jackson, the CEO, and I spoke. An eclectic array of people came in support, from David Steele to Peter Gabriel. As I walked out of the press conference to help with a photo-shoot outside, an Irish voice assailed me.

'Where's Richard?'

'He's just gone outside to do the photoshoot. I'll take you there.'

He held up a packet of Mates condoms.

'Is he showing these unwrapped?'

'Not to my knowledge.'

'For f***'s sake, that's what we need.'

He bit into a wrapped condom and tore one out, leaving it dangling as we approached the photographers.

It was Bob Geldof. I was reminded of the moment when he got angry in Live Aid two years earlier…

'Don't go to the pub tonight, please. Stay in and give us the money. There are people dying now [smashing the desk with his fist] so give us the money.'

This is when people really started to open their wallets.

In a more modest way than Live Aid, the Mates campaign did what the government and the establishment would never do. It confronted issues head-on. It understood and sympathetically exposed the barriers to behaviour change. It was fresh, unstuffy, inclusive and warm; a combination I have always tried to bring to social campaigns and a combination of qualities that was the antithesis to Thatcher herself.

Tony Blair arrives in Downing Street in 1997.

Chapter 3

Blair's panic about the Giving Age

WHAT IS THE LABOUR Party? To many, it is the party of labour, of the working man and woman, born originally out of the dignity and needs of those who predominantly worked with their hands.

It is the party of the NHS, free to everyone at the point of use; of the best possible education for all; of equality and social mobility; of improving the lot of the poor and vulnerable.

It is the party that protects the worker against exploitation by his or her bosses.

If you are a builder, a miner, a factory worker, a plumber or electrician, a nurse or a teacher, everyone understands what you do and have achieved at the end of a working day. It is tangible, measurable and it makes a clear and valuable contribution to society. A party that represents such people represents the honest toil on which we all rely.

Why then, when so much need, morality and justice belong to one party, does it need to reinvent itself as 'New Labour'?

The answer to this fundamental question is either 'no reason' or 'many reasons', depending on your point of view.

If you subscribe to the 'many reasons' point of view, then these reasons include the demonisation of the unions, principally by Thatcher, but sometimes by union leaders and members themselves; the subsequent castration of those unions; the effect of letting people buy their own council houses, thus creating more property-owning and more conservative voters; the automation of much manual labour and the spread of education, so that more jobs become intellectual/mental rather than physical/a trade; the general rise in living standards leading to gentrification.

The traditional power base of Labour dwindled as the UK population became more bourgeois, whilst its leadership remained wedded to the old ways and often the hard left. Then arose a team – Blair, Brown, Mandelson, Campbell

– and a way forward for Labour, inspired partly by the Democrat Party in the US, and specifically Bill Clinton. This idea sought to combine the social justice of the Labour movement with the prudent economic management usually associated with the right: 'New Labour'.

This concept – the 'Third Way' – when viewed through a flattering prism, is a combination of the best of two political traditions, to form a hybrid that is stronger and more advanced than either. It is a logical evolution to serve a more homogenous and less class-defined society.

Viewed another way, however, New Labour was a muddying of political intent destined to be full of contradictions and to ultimately fail.

If one took a philosophical view of twentieth-century British politics, we have voted in Labour governments to increase equality and to invest state money in hospitals and schools and public transport, and then a Tory government to rein in the state, increase efficiency and promote business.

These two parties have swapped power, as a substantial number of swing voters have perceived different needs. This has created a fairly constant pendulum-swing between left and right, like a form of arable crop rotation that maximises the land.

Clear differences of intent have presented clear choices to us as an electorate.

Arguably, the first example of a 'Third Way' was the Social Democrats, set up by the so-called Gang of Four. This failed to get lasting traction, split the left and ultimately became part of the Liberal Democrats.

Some would argue that as parties have all leant towards a middle ground we have lost ideology and increased confusion.

Anyway, New Labour was the phoenix of the Labour Party, born out of, and arguably only permitted by, the disasters and misjudgements of the Michael Foot and Neil Kinnock election campaigns.

Later, the Big Society as a concept was 'New Tory' in all but name; another 'Third Way', another attempt to create hybrid politics.

New Labour ran deeper, was much more intellectually robust and widely articulated, and found its time. It lasted several years and won three elections. The Big Society barely lasted two years and failed to win an outright election victory. It could still have great validity if properly executed, but more of that anon…

People talk of Blair ironically being the heir to Thatcher but Cameron is very much the heir to Blair. When Blair made his final Commons appearance, Cameron immediately rose to his feet and encouraged his somewhat reluctant party to do the same.

Like many people, I was very excited by Tony Blair. He was young, good-looking, intelligent and a brilliant public speaker. There was more than a touch of the JFK about him. Coming from a middle-class background myself, I wasn't hot under the collar about his Islington coterie. Indeed, he resolved for me a dilemma, as perhaps he did for others. He enabled me to think of people with my background as potentially at the heart of the Labour Party, whose ideology and purpose I admired.

When Tony Blair won the election and made his triumphal entrance into Downing Street, tracked by helicopters, I, like many others, felt the thrill of a new era, a new style of politics, a potentially more united country.

In his speech to the Labour Party in 1997, Tony Blair said the following:

> Our new society will have the same values as ever. It should be a compassionate society, but it is compassion with a hard edge. A strong society cannot be built on soft choices. It means fundamental reform of our welfare state, of the deal between citizen and society…
>
> Believe in us as much as we believe in you. Give just as much to our country as we intend to give. Give your all. Make this the Giving Age.
>
> On 1 May 1997, it wasn't just the Tories who were defeated. Cynicism was defeated. Fear of change was defeated. Fear itself was defeated. Did I not say it would be a battle of hope against fear? On 1 May 1997, fear lost. Hope won. The Giving Age began.
>
> Now make the good that is in the heart of each of us serve the good of all. Give to our country the gift of our energy, our ideas, our hopes, our talents. Britain, head and heart, can be unbeatable. That is the Britain I offer you. That is the Britain that together can be ours.

There is much of interest in this speech when examined a decade and a half later.

Firstly, Blair's new 'deal between citizen and society' is the fundamental basis of the 'Big Society' concept that David Cameron would introduce a decade later.

Secondly, there are strong, derivative echoes of Roosevelt's 'New Deal' and JFK's 'Ask not what your country can do for you, but what you can do for your country', albeit in a weaker form.

One should never underestimate the importance of American presidential charisma in what drove Tony Blair. Clinton was an idol but Blair was also all too ready to play 'younger brother' to George Bush. How differently Blair might have behaved if he'd been paired with Al Gore. World events would hopefully have taken a more positive turn.

Thirdly, the seeds of Blair's later downfall are all in this speech: the messianic, overblown statement that 'Fear itself was defeated', also derivative of 'We have nothing to fear but fear itself' and his reference to himself as a kind of prophet: 'Did I not say…?'

If Blair had not seen himself as a prophetic change-maker, with a religious or quasi-religious justification to his actions, he might not have seen facts, or unproven facts, as simply trivial hurdles to leap. Instead, he illegally invaded Iraq.

There were many powerful and specific ideas in Blair's speech and in his opening programme of policies, but the Giving Age was rather vague and all-encompassing, a politician's rather haphazardly conceived Jerusalem.

Perhaps it was no surprise that several months later, little had been done that tangibly epitomised this idea. For this reason, in 1998, a small group of people was asked to look at ideas that could turn this vision into something tangible.

Jane Tewson was the co-founder of Comic Relief. Jane is a fearless pioneer of philanthropic ideas, constantly challenging herself and others. She was close to, and greatly respected by, Gordon Brown. New Labour had understandably taken her to their bosom.

I knew Jane via her Comic Relief co-founder, Richard Curtis. I had taken over as President of the Oxford Etceteras, the Oxford equivalent of the Cambridge Footlights, from Richard and Rowan Atkinson. We stayed in touch and when Jane and Richard set up Comic Relief, I used my advertising knowledge and contacts to help secure their early corporate sponsors. I am very proud to have subsequently worked as an advisor on Comic Relief, albeit in a minor way, for twenty-five years.

When Jane was asked to bring the Giving Age to life, she asked me to join a small think tank. The other members of the group included Alan Parker, not the film director who had directed some New Labour party political broadcasts, but his namesake who ran the influential and successful Brunswick PR agency.

Alan is the son of Sir Peter Parker, ex-chairman of British Rail. The Parkers are a powerful business family and Alan had become one of New Labour's favourite 'masters of PR' or 'spin-doctors'. Alan has very generously and quietly supported a number of charities such as Pilotlight, also set up by Jane Tewson and Fiona Halton.

I suspect that Brunswick's links to many powerful

individuals and companies in the City and financial services made Alan Parker particularly interesting, especially to Mandelson. New Labour's love of, and 'intensely relaxed' attitude towards, the rich became more and more apparent.

Also in the group was Paul Weiland, the most consistently decorated and admired director of television commercials in the UK, especially those of a polished, comic nature: think 'Happiness is a cigar called Hamlet', 'Heineken refreshes the parts other beers cannot reach' and many more besides. Finally, there was MT Rainey, another advertising luminary later to become a social entrepreneur. She later set up the excellent horsesmouth.co.uk, a means of people mentoring others online.

We were thus a very communications-heavy group but we also had a track record of getting things done, and done in a compelling way. We were all strong contributors to Comic Relief.

Comic Relief is an odd but beguiling and rewarding idea: cry with laughter then cry immediately afterwards at poverty, confront it, give money and change things. In one sense it's the classic catharsis of Greek tragedy but with a potentially happy ending.

We see celebrities reduced to impotence and disbelief in Africa. We get angry at the injustice, side with their anger. We laugh at the collective recognition of the Comic Relief parodies: the basis of all comedy and humanity. We give small amounts, with millions of other people, and feel a particular surge of collective power.

Companies and individuals compete with each other to give substantial amounts to Comic Relief. We all compete with the previous year's Comic Relief total to try to beat it. We fight the common enemy of injustice that has been thrust vividly in our face. We are thanked and feel rewarded for giving.

Comic Relief has become the biggest single fundraising event in the world. It was hoped that we could create new, compelling ideas of this ilk for Tony Blair and New Labour.

What added extra scale, but also peril, to this challenge from the PM was a certain forthcoming event called the millennium. The dawning of another century is significant enough, but that of a new millennium is de facto rare. Planning for the year 2000 began as early as 1995, at least in political circles.

However, the enormity of a huge date and of equally huge public expectations is potentially suffocating to anything creative and innovative. Creativity usually flourishes away from the spotlight, in a playpen of trust and privacy and experiment – it certainly withers at the touch of a politician seeking to use it for his or her advantage. This, amongst other things, was to kill the Dome project.

The Millennium Dome, another good intention that ended sadly, partly framed our meeting with Blair and Mandelson. New Labour considerably expanded John Major's original plan for a re-run of the Festival of Britain to celebrate the third millennium. Just before its opening, Tony Blair claimed the Millennium Dome would be 'a triumph of confidence over cynicism, boldness over blandness, excellence over mediocrity'. Sadly, things didn't go to plan.

In 1997, I was working at the BBC as their marketing advisor, trying to ensure that marketing was implemented in the right way: to support public service broadcasting and to strengthen the hand of programme-makers, not weaken it. However, I had also been doing some research for the Millennium Dome and trying to help Jennie Page, the chief executive of the New Millennium Experience Company, create a coherent and successful project.

When I started to work on the Millennium Dome, I met up with Gary Withers, the unique founder of an extraordinary company, which defined itself by being called 'Imagination'. If you want the best staged event or exhibition, Imagination was and is an excellent first port of call. They have staged VIP dinners on the Great Wall of China and in the Forbidden City, flooding the courtyards and dyeing them with a carefully chosen ink to maximise the reflections by night. Need I say more? With Imagination, you get both soaring scale and attention to detail.

Gary was effectively the creative director of the Dome. He greeted me with the words 'Thank God you're here. Someone with a bit of sense!' He proceeded to show me the ideas for the Dome show and some of the Dome zones on beautiful scale models. The ideas for the show included giving the audience white T-shirts to wear so that they would become a kind of giant screen on which images could be projected. There were also plans for the parts of the auditorium to move round, changing permutation and perspective. It was impressive and ambitious in equal measure.

Gary significantly employed one person full-time, eight to ten hours a day, to file every single piece of paper associated with the Dome, from memos and letters to budgets and plans. He was always a meticulous note-keeper but took this to new heights because he knew it would all end in complicated disputes, especially when the government got so heavily involved. Sadly, his prediction was all too accurate.

I created ten to twelve key themes for the Dome with Gary and Jennie Page's team and then brought them alive in stimulus boards with provocative words and images. Because we wanted true opinions, I suggested that we dispensed with the usual focus group concept of eight demographically similar strangers per discussion and replaced them with groups of people who actually knew each other.

We had a couple of groups of schoolchildren from the same classes; a group of research scientists who worked in the same lab; a group of young men who played football together on a Saturday; and so on. Real opinions are forged at work, in clubs and pubs, at school, not in focus groups.

The results of our research were very uplifting and consistent. The public wanted ideas that were stimulating and provocative, not lowbrow and easy. Had the findings been followed through, the Dome would have been coherent, interesting, possibly a great success.

I attended a few meetings with Jennie Page and the boards of big companies who were potential sponsors, such as Sainsbury's. They agreed that they would pitch a zone or exhibition they could sponsor at a level that would educate and entertain the public rather than being crassly commercial.

Thus, Sainsbury's might sponsor an interactive exhibition about 'How the food on our plate reflects our changing world' rather than 'Sainsbury's: the 21st-century supermarket'. They were happy to contemplate this, as long as all sponsors consistently followed it through and no one was given blatant name-checks. Sadly, this wasn't always the case.

Mandelson and then Lord Falconer, as ministers for the millennium, interfered in a largely unproductive way with the Dome. There were many faults, including not following through a consistent vision and plan; sacking too many creative directors and using Jennie Page as a fall guy by firing her two months after opening; unrealistic targets of twelve million visitors in a year and opening only for a single year rather than two, which would have allowed greater payback; not giving the Dome a more resilient, longer-lasting structure when it would have possible to so do for comparatively little extra cost. As Basil Fawlty once memorably said, 'Yes, but apart from that, is everything OK?'

The known structure and globalism of the Olympics created good soil for Danny Boyle and his opening ceremony. His brilliant ability to define the quintessentially British and enjoy its eclecticism was something the Dome could have achieved, but never did. By the time we got to Boyle, politicians had learnt not to interfere with creative projects.

We were starting to deal with some of these ambitions

and tensions around the Dome when Jane Tewson called me into this project to answer Blair's ambitious brief, called 'ONE20'. The name encapsulated the idea that we could get a large section of the population to volunteer at least once a month: one day out of every twenty working days. 'We dream of a society where giving time to help others is normal, more normal in fact than giving money. Not everyone has money, but everyone has time; and everyone has something to give.'

The idea was that ONE20 would work in partnership with broadcasters to create motivational programmes that rebranded volunteering as fun, sharing, accessible and rewarding. It would work in conjunction with 200 local community focal points or hubs to create a supply chain of local opportunities for giving. We also wanted to distribute to every household in the UK an inspired and inspiring guide to how people could give time in their neighbourhood.

The idea was to build awareness of the campaign through 1999 and bring it to fruition from 2000 onwards. We wanted to use the symbolism of a new millennium but also the power of the seasons in drawing people into the movement.

One of my ideas was to ask people to make a midwinter resolution, on the winter solstice, the shortest and darkest day of the year, to volunteer over the coming year. This would be symbolised by people lighting torches and beacons in an interconnected chain across the UK: something big enough to be seen from space.

This would then move towards a celebration of all that

had been achieved through such volunteering on Midsummer Day 2000 through street parties up and down the land. This seasonal pattern of midwinter resolution and midsummer celebration would then continue each year, building up and celebrating volunteering throughout the UK. (Part of this idea finally came to fruition when I launched The Big Lunch almost a decade later.)

Our ideas were hugely symbolic, ambitious and difficult, but when, as a team, you've built Comic Relief, you have the BBC as a partner and the Prime Minister as your sponsor, everything seems feasible.

We discussed our ideas initially with Geoff Mulgan, who was head of Blair's policy unit. He filtered and vetted the ideas. When he felt we were ready, a date was set to present to the PM.

I arrived at Downing Street early by taxi and met the others. We had been into Downing Street a number of times in the preceding weeks to prepare, but this time it felt different as Geoff marched us up the famous road and steps. The same place can appear very differently according to circumstance. The street you work in feels different when you visit it on a weekend with your family; a film set from a parallel universe.

There was no security worth speaking of. It struck me that we could easily have smuggled in a weapon had we been so inclined. Having visited several times to prepare in the preceding weeks, we were now on some vetted list of people that were implicitly trusted, like the men with 'All Areas' passes on ugly lanyards that they wore with both forbearance and pride.

We were early and the PM was running late. We found ourselves standing in a waiting area outside the Cabinet Room next to the slim, tall and arrogant Peter Mandelson. He conspicuously ignored all of us even though he knew he was attending the same meeting. Alan Parker was the exception but even he only got short pleasantries.

I had never met Mandelson before but he just oozed schoolboy petulance, aloofness and a kind of histrionic indifference, as if he were a grand knight of the English theatre, which perhaps he should have been.

After a few minutes, the double doors of the Cabinet Room opened simultaneously and Tony Blair walked out with a visiting head of state. Power was palpable in their brisk walk. Eyes were straight ahead or for each other even though other dignitaries circled round. Downing Street was suddenly filled with one of its many VIP traffic jams.

I felt the frisson of rubbing shoulders with power but I also had a sense, from the dutiful faces that surrounded us, of the high-powered mundaneness of yet another meeting of two heads of state; the ordinariness of extraordinary things to the senior civil servants with their super-bright, graduate aspirants in tow.

Mandelson disappeared, doubtless to lobby Blair, and we were ushered into the Cabinet Room and left alone. We immediately felt like naughty schoolchildren let into the headmaster's study.

In between the press conferences, parties and dramas, the Downing Street rooms are sprinkled with the delicate and patient ticking of beautiful clocks. I examined a few of them. Perhaps in these peaceful moments, the best ideas and policies are forged, the true listening of diplomacy takes place and the complexities of briefing papers are read and properly ingested. The rest is theatre.

I took in the proportions of the room. Oddly placed pillars at one end have been used to support an extension, giving the room a curious asymmetry. It almost has the appearance of a room yet to be finished, perhaps appropriately, as the business of government *is* never finished.

The Prime Minister always sits in front of the fireplace in the central chair and the rest of the Cabinet table is a long, extended and tapering oval to maximise a sense of inclusion. Of course, Cabinets have got bigger and bigger to the point where it almost takes them longer to sit down than to have the meeting.

I picked up the silver candlesticks on the Cabinet table to see how heavy they were and half-feared an alarm going off. Light, including candlelight, was a key theme in the millennium part of our presentation and I was struck by the possibility of using one of these candlesticks as a prop. In my nervous excitement I had forgotten how inappropriate this would be: handling a piece of state history to simply make a point. Not quite Heseltine and the Mace but disrespectful nonetheless!

We all gazed round to see if there were any cameras

observing our pranks. We couldn't see any. After a few minutes the door opened and in came Tony Blair, followed by Jonathan Powell, his head of staff and one of three remarkable brothers – Charles, a key member of Thatcher's inner sanctum, and Chris, CEO of an ad agency and well known to me – plus Geoff Mulgan and Peter Mandelson and a secretary to record matters.

Blair came round to our side of the Cabinet table and introduced himself to each of us individually. His manners were impeccable. We all settled and I was struck by how penetratingly blue Blair's eyes really were. It was well known of him and was later to be demonised in Tory posters. He was aflame with self-aware charisma.

Throughout our presentations, Mandelson rocked back and forth on his chair and even passed a note behind Blair's back to Powell at one point like a naughty schoolboy. He made it very clear in his body language that he was absolutely nestled in the bosom of power and able to be his own Machiavellian self without the headmaster's restrictions.

The presentations went well and interested questions followed. Then Blair, who had been largely quiet, summed up the key points with the succinctness of a fine barrister. Mulgan summarised next steps and Blair came round the table and said goodbye to all of us, using our correct first names even though he had only heard them once. It was impressive and yet, even at the time, I felt he was very aware that we would all recount this impressive performance to many others beyond that room. Indeed, we have and I am doing it now.

After he left, we all collapsed in a state of relaxed euphoria. It had gone well. Our points had struck home.

The tangible idea that prevailed from these conversations was based on an American concept called 'time dollars'. It is built on the concept of time as the most important currency, a powerful and true observation of life, and applying it to volunteering. More specifically, we wanted to set up a mechanism by which the time and skills that people were prepared to volunteer could be matched and brokered with the time that charities needed from volunteers. It would use the power of the internet and software to attract and place people.

In effect, it was a dating service for volunteering. As with all dating sites, you could be well-matched to your charity 'date' by specifying the skills you could offer and the type of cause and charities you most want to help. Paul Weiland came up with the beautifully simple name of 'TimeBank': volunteers put money in and charities can draw it out.

We also wanted to challenge the stuffy preconceptions of volunteering as something 'worthy' and prove its value as something life-enriching. We came up with a concept called 'reverse mentoring'. Put simply, if a capable middle-class professional spends an hour a week helping a disabled child swim, the child is mentoring the adult as much as vice versa. This is a peculiar and touching truth that we had all discovered, as have many others.

The real difficulties came with implementation, as is so often the case. When I was trying to get government funding for TimeBank, Fiona Halton, fellow Comic Reliefer and serial social entrepreneur, and I had to meet with Lord Falconer, distinguished barrister, later to be Lord Chancellor, and closest friend to the Blairs.

The beginning of our meeting was somewhat odd for me, as I had last encountered him wearing a pair of ill-fitting, flowery swimming shorts on a beach. I couldn't quite get this image of Falstaff in Hawaiian shorts out of my mind.

After presenting our core plan, he asked us what outputs from TimeBank we could measure. This at first seemed reasonable, until his wish-list grew from the obvious and acceptable – e.g. the number of people visiting the site and the number of hours volunteered – to how many people visited Citizens Advice Bureaux, and rather a lot in between.

Fiona and I pointed out that no one organisation could achieve such a scattergun of outcomes. Frustrated by this, he then insisted that we guarantee a percentage increase in volunteering up-front before we received any funding. We pointed out that it was very difficult to guarantee such figures in advance.

This was an early indication of a government that became obsessed with metrics as a mechanism of political credibility. Measurement is essential but damaging if it is pursued for its own sake. The distortion of behaviours within the NHS and the police to simply 'make the numbers' subsequently proved this danger, as has the constant levelling down of GCSE and A level grades, thus necessitating the introduction of A*s because As beame so commonplace.

All politicians want to prove progress. Barrister politicians go about it in a particular way.

I also had problems with the BBC. Alan Yentob had persuaded the governors, or so we had been told, to air our short film/interstitial for TimeBank on the BBC. We were, after all, trying to increase volunteering and strengthen civic society, a perfect fit with the BBC's public service ethos. We had booked airtime and the first spot was due to be aired on *EastEnders*, to give it maximum exposure.

I was then told, a few hours before the first slot, that some of the governors had concerns. Until that point, the BBC had only given airtime to its own charities: Comic Relief and Children in Need. They were worried that airing our films would open the floodgates to half the charities in the UK filing up to ask for their charities to be promoted. Most of our airtime was cancelled.

Despite these problems, TimeBank was launched and has achieved a great deal in the intervening years.

We didn't usher in a Giving Age any more or less than already existed. British philanthropy is rightly admired and highly developed. Societal change cannot be brought about by the sheer willpower of politicians. Rarely is it sudden and momentous.

It often starts with thousands of small actions and changes which feed like tributaries into streams, which, in turn, aided by growing awareness and commentary by journalists and opinion-formers, feed into fast-flowing rivers.

Societies change in a dramatic sense because of revolutions, wars, invasions, climate change, immigration, and technological and scientific advances from the railway to penicillin to the internet. Politicians need to learn that their role is topically central but sometimes societally peripheral or weak.

Change the World for a Fiver: the book that sold

1.5 million copies with Gordon Brown's assistance.

Chapter 4

Gordon Brown's 'everyday heroes'

A SENIOR CIVIL SERVANT WHO was regularly involved in meetings of the New Labour inner sanctum beautifully summarised what he perceived as the differences between Gordon Brown and Tony Blair in two versions of the same scenario.

A foreign head of state is due to meet Tony Blair first thing in the morning. In the late afternoon before the meeting, Blair asks for a briefing paper of no more than two sides of A4, with the key situation analysis – relevant recent history, political and trade issues, sensitivities – and the desired outcome of the meeting. This would be presented and discussed in a meeting no longer than half an hour. Happy, Blair would then spring up the steps to the Downing Street flat for a session of air guitar and tapas (I made this last bit up but it feels about right!).

A foreign head of state is due to meet Gordon Brown first thing in the morning. Early afternoon, Gordon asks for an in-depth analysis and possibly even one or two books on the country concerned. In the evening he has a long briefing session; starts to read one of the books; panics by 11 p.m. that he hasn't grasped enough detail on the subject and cancels the meeting.

There is a degree of comic hyperbole in the tales but there is no caricature without strong, originating features. This was the yin and yang at the top of New Labour. Brown was the intellectual heavyweight, obsessed with drilling down in depth, but often lacking the people skills to be a charismatic leader. Blair was the 'big picture' ideologue, happier with woods than trees, a consummate charmer and confident presenter even when he had to busk it.

It crudely spells out why they were such a good double-act and very interdependent, both in the heady planning years before power and in the early days at No. 10, when the relationship was still vital. Brown is John Lennon: difficult, taciturn and prone to bouts of anger but on his day brilliant, beguiling and a man of deep, powerful feelings. Blair is Paul McCartney: better looking, boyish, charming, effortlessly talented but always looking for approval, full of melodies and sound bites.

The stereotypes don't quite do them justice, of course, because Blair was capable of great depth and intellectual rigour and Brown could be a great presenter and very charming.

In his book *A Journey*, Tony Blair describes being at a friend's house, where the two had met to discuss who would take over as Labour leader following the sudden death of John Smith in 1994. The old house was being renovated and during the meeting, Nick Ryden, the owner of the house, left the leadership contenders alone to talk. At one point Gordon Brown went upstairs to the loo.

Fifteen minutes passed. Blair wondered what was going on. Then the house phone rang. The answerphone clicked in and then Gordon's voice boomed out: 'Tony, it's Gordon here. I am upstairs in the lavatory and I can't get out.'

The lavatory door had been replaced but no handle had been put on the inside. Blair went upstairs and shouted through the door, 'Withdraw from the contest or I'm leaving you in there.'

There is a lovely domesticity and humour about this, a touch of Laurel and Hardy that humanises both of them and brings them closely into view.

I remember going to a private evening to celebrate one of Comic Relief's significant anniversaries. Gordon Brown was the guest speaker. Rory Bremner, who was on sharp and incisive form, preceded him. He was once described in a review of his show with the Johns Bird and Fortune as the 'most effective opposition in Britain', which had more than a grain of truth in it. Bremner was doing a brilliant impersonation of Blair, and Gordon was rocking backwards and forwards on his chair shaking with laughter. This happily continued when he himself became Bremner's target.

Then Gordon got up to speak, and he did so without a note. He talked with gravitas, compassion and knowledge about poverty in the third world and deprivation in the UK as well as the achievements of Comic Relief. He ended with a quote about how we all rely on other hands to hold us and put us in the grave.

It was both inspiring and moving. He was a different kind of speaker in these relatively intimate surroundings: truly impressive and heartfelt. In big set-piece speeches he could also be inspiring but often talked in long, heavy, overwrought sentences: the speech-making equivalent of Baroque architecture.

I really got to know Gordon Brown through David Robinson. David is, along with Jane Tewson, the social reformer I have most admired in my professional life. He set up Community Links in the Borough of Newham, in London's East End in 1977.

Community Links supports over 50,000 vulnerable children, young people and adults every year, coping daily with the consequences of poverty and struggling with the causes.

Not just financial hardship, but poverty of experience and – perhaps most crushing – poverty of expectation.

The organisation is a catalyst for change and brings together support from business leaders, volunteers, funders, government and service users to tackle some of the country's most intractable problems and, in learning from that process, share knowledge and experience from the ground up. Indeed, one of the first tasks I did for David Robinson was to name a book *Ground Up*, in conscious opposition to being 'ground down' as so many impoverished people are.

Every year, for many years, Community Links published an Ideas Annual in which it gave innovative ideas gratis to the whole voluntary sector. This kind of generosity should be the norm but so rarely is. The voluntary sector can sadly be as political as any commercial sector: too many needs and not enough money.

David Robinson came to me with an idea. He had met with Nike to learn about the power of the well-marketed brand. Nike's famous 'Just Do It' ethos captivated him as it had many. Their belief that if you have a body you can be an athlete is empowering.

Theirs was a culture grounded in the exact knowledge of how the foot pronates and flexes as it runs, having been co-founded by Phil Knight, a middle-distance runner himself, who once ran a mile in four minutes and ten seconds and who did a paper on sports shoes for his master's in business administration. He wanted to use this knowledge not to be elitist but to be irreverent and break the rules about who should compete in sport, how and why. As a result, their internal mantra was the odd but memorable phrase 'Irreverence justified'.

David wanted to apply these branding and presentation techniques to everyday actions that anyone could undertake to make the world a better place, spearheading a movement called 'We Are What We Do'. This was based on Gandhi's famous edict that 'we must be the change we want to see in the world'. David approached me and I suggested that we had to edit the number of actions down to fifty, to make sure they were fun and rewarding and were presented in a way that would attract a normally sceptical to indifferent reader.

I decided to turn each action into a double-page 'ad' in a book and commissioned the best art directors and copywriters to bring them alive. The book was also designed to be a Swiss army knife for action, a toolkit on your coffee table, by containing seeds you could sow, things you could cut out and post to neighbours or people you admired, phrases in different languages and so on.

The result was a book called *Change the World for a Fiver*. It has now sold over 1.5 million copies in several languages. It got the best possible start in life courtesy of Gordon Brown. He hosted a breakfast at No. 11 on 4 September 2004 with a number of major booksellers and distributors and our small editorial team. This was my first close-up encounter with him.

On the way to breakfast, I anticipated something like Claridge's in a political setting, with silver salvers containing perfectly creamy scrambled eggs and fragrant wild mushrooms.

Instead, we were treated to bacon sandwiches: a tad difficult for someone who's kosher, but refreshingly informal: a working man's café meets the Chancellor of the Exchequer. There were faint echoes of beer and sandwiches for union leaders at No. 10 under Harold Wilson.

We sat at a round table in the No. 11 dining room and Gordon swept in, full of nervous energy, fighting to overcome relentless tiredness. His eyes, which give him so much trouble, were dark and hooded from poring over red boxes late at night. He tucked into a couple of bacon sandwiches straight away, grabbing them with the hands of a Dickensian orphan, clearly having been up since dawn. He managed the bacon sarnies with somewhat more aplomb than his successor and colleague, Mr Miliband, would several years later in New Covent Garden market.

I was struck by Brown's ruggedness, both of intellect and physical presence: the rugby-playing son of the manse. He listened carefully, smiled and laughed. After we had all said our piece about the book, he turned to the assembled CEOs of the country's biggest booksellers and said: 'Well, gentlemen and ladies, I am sure you would like to take the whole initial print run between you. Let's hear some commitments.'

We did hear them and Justin King, then newly appointed CEO of Sainsbury's, polished things off nicely by agreeing to take the final 30,000 copies. When power works, it works quickly.

The Chancellor left in a hurry but graciously and I was left struck by his honesty, forcefulness and desire to get things done.

Later, in 2007, a small group of us were asked to form an informal advisory group to Gordon on challenging social issues; a forerunner to what was to become the Council on Social Action.

He was complex and contradictory in these meetings. On the one hand, he spent time at the end of each meeting asking people about their mother's cancer or their daughter's problems at school, showing a perfect and impressive memory for peoples' personal circumstances. These were people who had been known to him for a while but even so, it was very impressive and heartfelt.

On another occasion, he arrived incredibly late and said, 'Sorry, I have only got half an hour. Is that OK?' Because nobody replied immediately, his tone rose quickly to anger. 'Well, is it?'

We nodded quickly and his temper cooled. I never forgot that quickness to anger, although I didn't ever see it again personally. However, I understood it to be borne out of exhaustion, overwork, guilt, concern and an inability to delegate and wasn't helped by his poor eyesight. The little email I received from him was written entirely in capitals to help him see properly, often without much punctuation, a passionate stream of consciousness.

One of the projects we worked on was the publication of a book called *Britain's Everyday Heroes*. It was a series of interviews Gordon conducted with people who did remarkable things on a quiet and everyday basis, the people who inspired him. This was a foretaste of his effort to reform the honours system to recognise more unsung heroes of their communities. Whilst he succeeded to an extent, the press still highlight the entertainers and sporting heroes who have been honoured which undermines such efforts.

One of our meetings was especially memorable. Gordon arrived late, as one comes to expect of people in power dealing with people who are not, and, almost before sitting down, asked the formidable question 'What can be done about knife crime?'

We were all slightly stunned, as we hadn't gathered to discuss this topic, but it was ever-present in the newspapers and clearly uppermost in his mind. We offered up some answers – knife amnesties; more community policemen on the beat of more ethnically varied backgrounds; stiffer jail sentences; ex-offender rehabilitation.

We also came to the honest conclusion that in the end the solution would take a generation at least. It requires people to be better, loving and more disciplined parents, even in the toughest of circumstances, so that they can raise the self-esteem of their children, giving them the mechanisms for rejecting violence. He warmed to the humanity and honesty of our answers whilst also showing the politician's frustration with the absence of short-term, ready-to-be-announced policies.

Later in the meeting, we were on another big subject: low voter turnout and lack of engagement with democracy. I asked him, 'Is it possible to break down my tax spend every year into constituent parts?'

He looked curious. 'What exactly do you mean?'

When the Chancellor of the Exchequer asks you this question, staring you straight in the eyes, you can feel your naïveté spreading like a blush, but I continued, hoping that my naïveté could also be strength.

'Could you tell me, or my household, that last year we spent, say, £1,600 on the NHS; £1,200 on education; £850 on defence etc. etc.? Could you do the equivalent for every household?'

'Yes, it's perfectly possible. We have the data and the software I'm sure. Why?'

'Because, tax is taken from people in anonymous blobs, percentages, before they even receive it. People don't even know what National Insurance pays for versus income tax. If people know how much they spend on each item, they will want value-for-money. They will have a point of view. They will become more engaged.'

'But it could be chaos, because people who don't have children resent paying for education. People who are passionately against the nuclear deterrent don't want to pay for it.'

'That's the price of involvement, though. If you want people to engage they need transparency and tangible things and price tags that relate back to them.'

He remained intrigued but resistant and I sensed in him an interesting tension between being in control of spending behind closed doors and opening it up to greater public involvement. His inability to let go, to delegate in a number of ways, was perhaps his greatest Achilles heel.

I gave the same idea to Francis Maude and Oliver Letwin years later when I was working with them on the Big Society. Now the coalition government is issuing annual tax summaries to each individual to tell them exactly how their taxes are spent.

Someone on a salary of £30,000, for example, will see that £1,663 of their money is spent on welfare, with £1,280 going to health, £892 going to education, £822 going to the state pension and £475 going on national debt interest.

I welcome the fact that my idea is finally being put into action but it looks as though the Tories are keen to do it only to highlight how much goes on welfare.

After this radical suggestion was originally delivered to Gordon Brown, the meeting ended and I exited the wrong way, ending up in the ground floor vestibule of No. 11 with a staircase ascending up to the private apartments. The sunlight was pouring in through the fanlight and it was unusually quiet. I suddenly jumped, realising I was not alone. A sole figure stood halfway up the stairs: Gordon Brown. He beamed and said, 'I am just waiting for my son to be brought down.'

The son in question was James Fraser, born in July 2006, his second son, later to be tragically diagnosed with cystic fibrosis. They had lost their first child, a daughter, Jennifer Jane, from a brain haemorrhage only a few days after she was born. John Macaulay was the older brother.

It was a very tender and unforgettable moment to see the

second most powerful man in the land taking a quiet moment out to hold his baby son.

In a later Council on Social Action meeting, when he was Prime Minister, I remember hearing the cries of 'Daddy, Daddy' as he left our room.

I recalled these moments when he left Downing Street for the last time, walking hand in hand with Sarah and the two boys. In the end, at its most fundamental, Downing Street, however elevated and public, is a home with families. If this could be felt more viscerally, more of the time, on both sides, we might have a more harmonious society; one in which top-to-bottom power seems shallow.

Gordon Brown talks about the Council on Social Action
at the Chain Reaction conference.

Chapter 5

Musical chairs and
the Council on
Social Action

WHEN HE FINALLY BECAME Prime Minister,
Gordon Brown wanted to gather together the
best social reformers and entrepreneurs and get
them to work with senior civil servants to find original and

cost-effective ways of solving society's toughest problems. He thus established the Council on Social Action, or COSA for short.

He announced the idea on the symbolically important date of 24 July, or 24/7. His vision was to build 'The Good and Active Society', an encapsulation that has subsequently been forgotten. It is, in retrospect, a far more accurate and superior call to action than the later and derivative Big Society, of which more anon.

Gordon's idea was that 24/7 should be a day to see, hear, reward and celebrate Britain's 'everyday heroes'. It could thus become an optimistic antidote to the dark dates of 9/11 and 7/7: the Twin Towers and London terrorist attacks.

More importantly, however, 24/7 was about a powerful principle: that only by an aggregation of small actions and one-to-one mentoring, performed by millions of people, every hour of every day, can we solve our tough, ingrained societal and environmental problems.

In addition to COSA, the PM announced a City Leaders programme and a global forum for social leaders.

The Council on Social Action was chaired by the PM but much of the organising work naturally fell to its vice chair David Robinson, who had co-conceived the idea. It was a large and formidable group: too large, in fact. When one added in all the government team and advisors there were twenty-five official members plus advisors and note-takers. Prior to its formation, we had to apply for selection and be scrutinised by the Cabinet Office.

Members included: Geoff Mulgan of the Young Foundation, founder of the Demos think tank and ex-head of the policy unit under Tony Blair; Julia Unwin, director of the Rowntree Foundation; David Thomlinson, the philanthropic CEO of Accenture; Sophi Tranchell, founder of Divine Chocolate, the fairtrade chocolate company co-owned by its cocoa farmers; Julia Ogilvy, founder of Project Scotland, using volunteering to transform the lives of young Scots; Rob Owen, CEO of St Giles Trust, an award-winning charity with multiple new ideas on reducing re-offending; and Tim Smit, co-founder of the Eden Project. These were just some of the social entrepreneurs involved, including myself.

On the government side, in addition to the PM, we had Phil Hope, the minister for the Third Sector, a department that Gordon Brown had created and named, in somewhat Soviet-era fashion, in 2005; Campbell Robb (a great swashbuckling name straight out of a Rabbie Burns poem), the first director general of the Office of the Third Sector (and probably the last, as it's a rather curious title).

There were also a number of individuals very close to Gordon Brown: Kirsty McNeill, tireless campaigner and one of the co-ordinators of 'Make Poverty History'; Oona King, broadcaster, journalist and campaigner; and Gila Sacks, youngest daughter of the then Chief Rabbi, who was a policy advisor in the Cabinet Office.

This is not an exhaustive list but you get the idea: an incredibly rich range of inventive talents, ready to ferment a cauldron of ideas.

Our first meeting was on 11 December 2007. We were seated in a large rectangle with tent cards to announce our names and credentials, in the largest formal entertaining room, at the back of the house, overlooking Horse Guards Parade.

We discussed our remit first in a rather formal, self-conscious way. I remember David Robinson seeming much more at ease than most. He knew Gordon Brown well enough to not feel intimidated and his fluency was vital as the clutch and gear-change between political power, civil service protocol and social enterprise.

The Prime Minister entered with TV camera crews in tow. In a moment we all moved from peeping from the wings to being on the stage. The PM came round and shook all our hands personally. I felt a slightly queasy sense that gathering us all together in front of the cameras was a political statement in itself. There was also, of course, a feeling of immense pride. Whilst to us the cameras were a distorting effect on behaviour, to Gordon Brown they were an ever-present irritant, akin to accepting that a neighbouring house will always look directly into your living room.

The PM talked a lot about the power of one-to-one relationships to help even the most vulnerable and disadvantaged people and to solve our toughest societal problems. We were off and running.

COSA created some very powerful ideas including social impact bonds: a contract with the public sector in which a commitment is made to pay for improved social outcomes that result in public sector saving. New and innovative programmes have potential for success, but often have trouble securing government funding because it can be hard to rigorously prove their effectiveness.

This form of financing allows the government to partner with innovative and effective service providers and, if necessary, private foundations or other investors willing to cover the upfront costs and take on some of the risk. This allows government to expand promising programmes, whilst assuring that taxpayers will not pay for the programmes unless they demonstrate success in achieving the desired outcomes.

COSA also set up the 'Global Forum for the exchange of Social Ideas', which I was asked, as the communications man, to brand rather more succinctly. When I was at Oxford, I had helped Simon Baron-Cohen, now Professor of Developmental Psychopathology at the University of Cambridge and a renowned specialist in autism, to set up a student magazine called *Mandrake*: 'a magazine for the international collision of ideas'. Only utterly pretentious and over-confident students could possibly create such a grandiose title and I blush to recollect!

With that folly (albeit an interesting folly) still ringing in my ears, I wanted to find a name that was exciting but not hyperbolic. I conceived the name, or rather chose the colloquialism of, 'Chain Reaction'. It was a name that occurred to me whilst walking through a Downing Street reception and seeing the baton-pass of ideas, favours and parcels of power between excited participants. Everyone liked it and we got on with staging the events.

COSA also helped with the launch of The Big Lunch, of which more in the next chapter, and it set up its own awards scheme to acknowledge and reward social entrepreneurs.

Side by side:
a report setting out the Council on
Social Action's work on one-to-one

The Council on Social Action's report on the power of one-to-one relationships in solving social problems.

At the heart of COSA's work was the idea that one-to-one mentoring was the key to cracking many ingrained social problems. Studies had shown, for example, that the most chaotic and troubled families could cost the state £300,000 a year. This was partly because so many of them were dealt with by a ridiculous number of interventions, by different government departments working in silos. Instead, one dedicated person could act as the conduit for all help offered by government. We wanted each and every civil servant to make personal contact with someone whose lives their jobs touched, whether they were prisoners, the disabled, victims of crimes, postmen, social workers or nurses.

In addition to wanting a universal mentoring scheme in schools, we wanted to have one-to-one mentors in the NHS, in the police and in social service. We wanted to humanise public services and emphasise that 'the best youth workers, teachers, health visitors don't seek to control people, or make them dependent, but to be the influence in the lives of others that makes them free'.

Yet despite these substantial achievements, there were a number of curious, indeed comic, aspects of the meetings that took place over COSA's two-year lifespan.

The first folly was that it had been decided, for reasons that no one could quite fathom, that in each of the two-hour meetings, the Prime Minister would come in for an hour after half an hour of the meeting had lapsed, and then leave half an hour before the meeting ended. Credit where it's due, it takes skill to make a decision this disruptive and inefficient. The first half an hour was spent getting ready for the PM and for the last half an hour everyone slumped into a demob-happy state, like sixth-formers after the headmaster finishes his visit to the common room.

In addition, the difference between the entrepreneur and the civil servant was perfectly epitomised when David Robinson turned up at Downing Street to run a sub-committee of COSA and asked if he could just have a circle of chairs and no table. The civil servants stared at him in disbelief, as if he was setting up some sort of bizarre, brainwashing cult in the centre of power. He explained that he wanted an informal brainstorming. Reluctantly they removed the table for him.

He returned a few weeks later to run a much bigger and formal COSA meeting and found two long rows of chairs and no table. He spoke to the members of staff on duty: 'Can I have a few tables please?' They again looked at him in disbelief and with some degree of hurt. 'But we've got you down in our notes as the no-table man!' David drew breath and tried not to sound as if he was lecturing three-year-olds. 'Sometimes I have formal meetings and I need tables and tent cards and minutes. At other times, I just want to be informal and do a brainstorming.'

They reluctantly put out the tables and left shaking their heads at this alien force called 'the Brainstormer'. Flexibility is not the core strength of the civil service.

Another fascinating point of contrast between the civil service and us was on the subject of meeting minutes. A designated member of our group – the social entrepreneurs

– would write up the notes in twenty-four hours and submit them to the Cabinet Office. A number of weeks later, a noticeably blander and longer document would be sent back with all the interesting rough edges taken out and anything close to a definite government commitment surgically excised.

Because the Prime Minister chaired these meetings, they had to be kept carefully as official records. We all understood this. However, the level of caution they displayed became extraordinary. Phil Hope, the Minister for the Third Sector, announced at one meeting that to light a path for other ministers and members of the government, he would volunteer for a few hours a week. In fact, he had already started to mentor an ex-offender through the St Giles Trust. We put this fact in the minutes. They took it out. We asked for it to be put back in.

'We can't be seen to minute that the minister is doing something in case he doesn't have the time to do it.'

'But he's already doing it and has done so for several weeks!'

'Nevertheless, he might not be able to continue to do it…'

I can vouch for the accuracy of *Yes, Prime Minister*!

A new level of farce was reached in one of the later COSA meetings. The night before one of our big meetings, we had been phoned to ask us to come in much earlier than planned because Gordon Brown had an urgent meeting to attend afterwards. We duly turned up at No. 10 at 8 a.m.

We had breakfast in the Cabinet Room and a quick chat amongst ourselves. Then more breakfast and another chat. No explanation was forthcoming. Finally, we were asked to sit down.

A member of the PM's team came in to explain: 'The Prime Minister sadly cannot join you after all, but a colleague is coming to chair the meeting. He apologises and promises that he will definitely attend the next meeting in full.'

We wait several more minutes and then suddenly, in the manner of a Feydeau farce, a dishevelled figure suddenly appeared, as if an actor thrown onto a stage against his will. He looked round with a degree of stage fright. 'Oh, hello. This must be … err…'

'The Council on Social Action.'

'Err … Yes, that's it. So, tell me what you do again.'

It was Ed Miliband MP, at that time a fairly obscure Brownite supporter living in the shadow of his Foreign Secretary elder brother. We appeared at the time to have been given 'the wrong Miliband'. History has yet to tell us if this assumption was right.

After we explained our remit to him, he got on with the job and to be fair, whilst somewhat nervous, he synthesised the content well.

All was going swimmingly until the Cabinet door creaked open and Gordon Brown entered awkwardly and unexpectedly. Seeing the 'I thought you were in another meeting' expression on all our faces, the PM stuttered: 'I just came in to say that I am sorry not to be with you because I'm somewhere else. But you're in good hands with Ed.'

He gazed down the Cabinet table to where Ed Miliband was sitting in the Prime Minister's chair in front of the fireplace at the centre of the extended oval Cabinet table. The tent card 'The Prime Minister' was in front of Miliband. He picked it up and threw it down the table. 'Oops. I don't want you to think I'm planning a coup!'

It was a lovely act of witty banter and saved the day ... just.

It strikes me, now that Gordon Brown has long left office and Miliband is the post-fratricide leader of the Labour Party, that the Cabinet Room is the most famous example of musical chairs on record.

This bizarre mixture of mould-breaking ideas and extraordinary ineptitude continued until the last meeting of COSA.

We were all supposed to have a group photograph with the PM. It didn't happen. Instead, when he came in halfway through the meeting, a photographer came in to do some reportage shots of just him in situ. Not guaranteed to make the rest of us feel acknowledged, and it wasn't as if the world was starved of pictures of Gordon Brown.

Tim Smit always looked as if he'd just come off an allotment, with an untidy haystack of hair and clothes that sported remnants of that day's meals. This occasion was no exception. After the PM had departed, someone said, in a suitably droll manner, 'Shame about the group photo, especially when you've made such an effort, Tim!'

As the PM left, he thanked us all profusely for our work and said, 'We were, as you know, planning to have a reception for you. Unfortunately, there's been some confusion and we have double-booked you with a Muslim group. Please, however, feel free to join in with their drinks.'

Most of COSA chose not to take on this eclectic experience,

possibly due to the likely absence of alcohol, but a few of us did venture in, if only out of curiosity. I found myself standing next to Sarah Brown, whom I knew a little from her kind hosting of an event for the Pilotlight charity at No. 10 that year. I like and admire her a lot from the little I have encountered her: she is utterly down to earth, with clear and strong opinions.

'How many of these receptions do you do in an average day?' I asked her.

'Typically, two or three and you only get a few minutes' briefing sometimes.'

'It must feel like repertory theatre.'

'Got it in one.'

Looking back on COSA meetings, they were in many ways superior to what subsequently happened with the Big Society. They systematically explored a manageable number of ideas in depth and through a wise use of sub-groups who reported back to the council.

They looked at international best practice (although the Big Society did this in a few areas such as participatory budgeting). The role of charities and volunteers was recognised and heralded from the beginning, whereas the Big Society appeared to borrow their clothing without acknowledging the original owner.

COSA was realistic about how tough the ingrained problems are. The government acknowledged the vital role to be played by digital and social media and encouraged innovation in this arena. COSA also asked the City to make a tangible contribution to society almost a year before the Lehmann Brothers collapse on 15 September 2008 and all that followed with the financial crisis. COSA was inclusive and prescient in many ways.

Tim Smit and Paul Twivy launching The Big Lunch in 2009.

Chapter 6

The Big Lunch and Downing Street's neighbours

WHEN WE THINK OF Downing Street, we don't think of neighbours, except the Chancellor and Prime Minister occasionally swapping flats between 10 and 11, based on the size of their families and, presumably, their egos. When we think of its neighbourhood, we think only of the political village of Westminster. It is cut adrift from normal life on an island of its own power. Yet my next visit was an attempt to change that, to link it to a new kind of constituency.

It started with several pints of red wine shared between Tim Smit and I in that heady excitement of first encountering a kindred spirit. Tim Smit is an ever-curious and eccentric innovator, a restless spirit, fascinating if sometimes frustrating and wilfully different. He can fill a room but can equally overshadow or ignore a team. He relies on collaboration yet isn't a natural collaborator.

The Eden Project is inspiring in its teaching but has sometimes been chaotic behind the scenes despite the best efforts of some of its senior team. Tim's achievements have required unreasonableness and unreasonableness has its dark side. His first career was in the music business as a songwriter and producer. He then decided on a lifestyle change and moved to Cornwall with his family. There he discovered the Lost Gardens of Heligan and how to be lead singer of his own band.

Sixteen of Heligan's twenty-two gardeners were killed in the First World War. The garden became neglected and then untouched and overgrown for decades after it was separated from its house and estate. There is a Dickensian quality to finding this overgrown, partly walled garden, lost in time, opening its creaking doors and then restoring it back to its former glory. This is precisely what Tim and a group of fellow enthusiasts did: Miss Havisham meets horticulture.

Tim then founded and led the Eden Project, creating two extraordinary biomes and much more besides, in a disused clay pit in Bodelva. In many ways, the Eden Project has been the most successful and enduring millennium project, and certainly delivers the most important message. The Eden Project provides a visceral education about the inter-dependence of plants and people.

What Tim has always understood is the importance of theatre and storytelling in this process. He has brought show business to environmental education and thereby greatly extended its reach without in any sense trivialising it. The name Eden itself weaves a spell: the lost, original state of a world created beautiful, the lost innocence of humanity.

One example epitomises their approach. Schoolchildren visiting Eden have sometimes been asked to fill a pitcher with water and carry it up to the top of Eden's pit and back down again. Whilst still exhausted, they are told to imagine that journey but many times longer as the morning routine of over a billion people every day. They never forget it. As Confucius said, 'I hear and I forget. I see and I remember. I do and I understand.'

Jane Tewson always insisted that people visit Comic Relief projects before they get involved for precisely this reason. This created a core of committed talent.

Eden has attracted over twelve million people since its opening in 2000. It has put over £1 billion into the frail Cornish economy and placed the environment firmly at the centre of our gaze.

I met Tim originally because I was exploring the possibilities of enhancing a botanical drink for a client. I knew that

Eden had made botanicals more compelling than anyone else and so I went to learn. The botanical drink evolution never happened but something far more significant did.

Tim and I originally talked about how Eden, although incredibly successful, was still fundamentally a kind of 'environmental theme park' in the south west of England. We discussed how it could become more pervasive in its influence. Could we, for example, inspire people throughout the UK to put new environmental ideas into practice in their own 'local Edens'?

To Tim, the key, missing ingredient in environmental action was, and is, stronger communities. Much is happening at micro, individual household level, from recycling to better insulation, from smart meters to smaller and hybrid cars. Much is supposed to be happening at macro level: international agreements between governments and NGOs such as the Kyoto Protocol. The meat missing in the sandwich is at street and neighbourhood level. It is at this level that people can share resources such as water, power, tools and transport. In the process, they re-discover solidarity as well as saving resources.

Roger Graef, the legendary documentary filmmaker, says that the key to excellent documentaries is to spot 'the significant detail'. Tim Smit has an eye for the same thing. He often talks about the waste of one street having 100 lawnmowers used only a few hours a year each, or 100 power drills used only a few minutes a year apiece. A communal sharing would make much more sense. This is merely one detail in a whole series of neighbourly opportunities ranging from shared transport to recycled toys, clothing and furnishings, to urban gardening and street-based social media.

It is interesting that a recent Nobel Prize winner proved that it is local farmers co-operating who have created the world's most efficient irrigation systems, not governments. Modern media have made us part of a global village of the impotent, in which we simply gaze helplessly at world events as they unfold. What we need is to live in communities and neighbourhoods in which we have an identity, a voice, and practical ideas, leverage.

Babies rely on the reactions on the faces of their parents and families to know that they are loved or even exist at all. Faces are their mirrors. If a baby cries and no one comes then that baby begins to feel traumatised. Why can't he or she conjure a loving face? Are they completely alone? If there is no effect, there can be no cause.

If there is no cause they are not corporeal merely an invisible spirit. The same is true with communities. We look for recognition in faces of those who live around us. If we don't find it, we lose a layer of identity.

I grew up in a village, at the tail end of thousands of years of local, agricultural life. Houses and cars were left unlocked. My parents never worried about where we were because we had an identity. We were seen. My children have grown up in a fairly respectable part of London and with lots of love and security, but still hurry up our street at night worried by anonymity, by the haunting stranger.

For all these reasons, Tim Smit and I share a passion for community, for the 'village-isation' of our cities. For me, some of the darkest aspects of our modern age, in Britain any way, are social isolation and loneliness (which are not the same but do heavily overlap).

In 2004, I was made redundant from my last job in advertising as chief strategic planning officer for Europe, Middle East & Africa of McCann Erickson (my business card was the size and shape of a baguette). I was forty-five. Advertising is an ageist profession and although I was more experienced, mature and efficient than ever before, I knew it would be very difficult to become re-employed. I was right.

As the father of five children this was depressing not to say frightening. So, I embarked on a portfolio career, possibly described as such because you spend a huge amount of time lugging around your 'portfolio' trying to pick up work. You're only ever a few steps away from feeling like a door-to-door salesman.

As with many people in this situation, my self-esteem plummeted. When I came back from the gym on a weekday, the children had gone to school and Gaby, my wife, had gone to pottery. The slam of the front door echoed into silence. As I walked upstairs to my study at the top of the house, I felt my heart sink.

The study looked out on our street: laid out in front me like a film set viewed from a crane. It often seemed ghostly in the way that only a road in a cold climate truly can. It got to the point when I panicked and wanted to phone Gaby to say: 'Don't leave me on my own. I don't know what I might do.' Irrational thoughts flashed through my head.

If I felt a panic of failure, an aching loneliness, despite having five wonderful children, a loving wife, a warm, extended family, supportive friends and all the advantages of a good education and reasonable wealth, I started to wonder how others with far less support in their lives must feel. It is salutary to remember that we are all only a few steps away from sleeping on the park bench, from sliding into an addiction. We are all both capable and vulnerable: my touchstone philosophy.

I started to think about how much loneliness there might be on our street. I remembered the stories from my Royal Mail clients of postmen finding people unconscious or dead, on the floors of their houses or flats, following days of neglect. No one had visited or knocked or worried, the only clue being the silent build-up of junk mail on the mat.

The opposite side of the coin of British tolerance and laissez-faire is the extraordinary ability to ignore what is in front of, or next to you – to build a thick wall of indifference that is sometimes shocking in its consequences. People have lived next door to domestic violence for many years, hearing it if not seeing it, and failed to report it.

People have been sexually molested or knifed on public transport and no one witnessing it has intervened. When the British fight for a dramatic cause we fight like hell. When we live continually with a cause next door however, we often ignore it. Neglecting people who are lonely is perhaps our most frequent crime.

As Ben Macintyre said in *The Times* in 2009: 'The appalling rapist who made his daughters pregnant … did not need to build an underground cell like Josef Fritzl in which to commit his crimes: he could rely instead on the thick walls of British reticence to hide the horror.'

One in ten British adults regularly experiences loneliness: over four million people. Recent estimates place the number of people aged over sixty-five who are often or always lonely at over one million. Two million people are on their own on Christmas Day and yet, in a large YouGov survey, only 25 per cent of 2,070 British adults thought they had a responsibility to keep in touch with older neighbours who might be lonely.

At Christmas, when I was a child, we always invited one or two older people who would otherwise be on their own. We also took a Christmas dinner with all the trimmings to the houses of those who couldn't get out. The delayed gratification of waiting for our best meal of the year, the bubbling-under resentment of not just being our family, was far outweighed by the sheer pleasure they felt and expressed at being with us. It was a defining aspect of my upbringing.

It is not just the elderly who are affected by loneliness: only 42 per cent of British 11-to-15-year-olds find their peers 'kind and helpful': the worst score of any developed country. We need to make isolation history, not just poverty.

Researchers looking at a demographic of 309,000 people found that those with stronger social relationships had an increased 50 per cent survival rate over others who are more isolated. This was consistent across factors including age, sex, health status and cause of death. Evidence shows that as a risk factor, loneliness and isolation is on a level comparable with smoking and alcohol consumption. It is more detrimental than physical inactivity and obesity.

Out of these passions to tackle isolation, to make communities closer and stronger, we wanted to create something that would capture the public's imagination. It needed to be simple, rewarding, fun.

Tim mentioned that he had an idea called simply 'The Big Lunch', an event in which as many people across the UK as possible sat down and had lunch with their neighbours on a single day. As soon as I heard it, I believed it could work and told him so. We agreed that I would set about making it happen.

There is a strong and vibrant tradition of street parties in the UK but mainly connected with royal jubilees or special, national commemorations. The memories are widespread and vivid like a postcard in the nation's mind. We wanted to build on but change this tradition. We wanted people to have street parties for the sake of all of us, a sort of 'Thanksgiving Day for neighbours'.

I started along the bumpy road of turning the idea into a reality and crafted the following vision…

Once a year, we want as many of the sixty-one million people in the UK as possible to simultaneously sit down to lunch together, with their neighbours, in the middle of their street, as a simple but profound act of community.

Everyone will be asked to personally grow or create a small gift for that lunch.

Britain would cease its toil, anxiety and loneliness and heal itself for a few crucial and uplifting hours. For three to four glorious hours, traffic would stop, technology would be switched off, and people would meet, eat, discuss, laugh, and feel hope.

In the weeks and months preceding the day itself, Britain's window-boxes, gardens, school playgrounds, allotments and even public parks would be given over to growing food and flowers for the occasion.

In homes and schools all over the country, people would create tablecloths, decorations, cushions, banners, murals, songs, jokes, stories, and pieces of street theatre for use on the day.

The day after, people will walk down their street and know someone in most windows. They will be able to wave rather than scurry face down in isolation.

It is especially important that those living in deprived urban estates and tower blocks are given the means of turning this into a reality.

It is vital that The Big Lunch belongs to everyone in the country and acts as a means of turning neighbourliness into a springboard for everyday actions in every community.

We want to hold it on a Sunday to maximise participation and build on the tradition of Sunday lunch.

It was a utopian vision but a powerful one. We didn't want it to be po-faced but to express what Tim Smit called 'The Rebel Yell': a positive outlet for our collective anger and rebellion. We sensed that may people were fed up with just working and consuming, with isolation and anxiety, feeling powerless in the face of issues ranging from street crime through to global warming.

We attracted a large number of powerful allies. Very early on, Royal Mail agreed to help us by, for example, franking every stamped envelope in the UK during the build-up to the day to raise awareness. Posties go out onto Britain's streets every day and witness neighbourliness and loneliness at first hand. Royal Mail delivers to 29 million addresses every day and employ almost 150,000 people to do so, of whom 80,000 pound the streets. They are a unique form of social glue. Our logo was stamped on a staggering 2 billion letters.

Eden's involvement and the 'grow your own' aspects of The Big Lunch attracted and excited the horticultural world: from the RHS to the National Trust. Celebrities such as Jamie Oliver and Hugh Fearnley-Whittingstall contributed recipes for the perfect street food. Hugh also launched an initiative called Landshare, whereby people with land to lend or share could be paired with people who wanted to grow but had no land.

Rosie Boycott was a good friend of Tim Smit and was passionate about urban and guerrilla gardening plus access to locally sourced, healthy food which she was already exploring with Boris Johnson: an initiative that became London

Food. I remember first visiting her house in Notting Hill which had the unmistakable air and trappings of someone who has been at the centre of public life for several decades. The signed, original sketch by John Lennon in her hallway was not surprising as the co-founder of Spare Rib in the society-exploding '60s, but it still took my breath away.

Boris Johnson himself was an early supporter of The Big Lunch and has remained so through the subsequent years, often appearing at our street parties with Barbara Windsor in a suitably pantomime duo and sweeping across road closure red tape with a sweep of his blond mane.

The Council on Social Action and Cabinet Office supported The Big Lunch, as did Hazel Blears and the Department for Communities and Local Government. The first time I met Hazel I wasn't sure whether to be more bowled over by her motorcycle leathers and helmet in the corner of the room, the shock of ginger hair on a postage stamp-sized figure, the gush of energy or her opening statement of 'I don't suppose you've ever been to Salford?' (Her constituency!)

However, getting corporate support wasn't so easy. As I had learned many years before with Comic Relief, to attract corporate partners, not simply sponsors (a crucial distinction, the former representing genuine involvement and the latter more of a name check in exchange for another kind of cheque) you need to find a genuine link between the brand's commercial objectives and the cause in hand.

This led me to Orange, the mould-breaking mobile telecoms and broadband company. Their brand built itself on the optimism of 'The future's bright, the future's Orange'. They were a brand based on communications and networking. They had also started to show an interest in new forms of volunteering by partnering a venture called 'Rock Corps', which incentivised young people to volunteer with the reward of exclusive rock concert tickets.

I had also worked for a while on a campaign with MasterCard, whose brand idea was that the best experiences are 'priceless' and 'for everything else there's MasterCard'. This is a refreshing combination of accepting that a credit card is utilitarian whilst what it enables can be vital. We suggested to them that strengthening communities was priceless and together we forged the thought: 'Turning our streets into neighbourhoods: Priceless.'

I also approached companies such as British Gas, specifically their New Energy division, set up to deliver carbon footprint reduction and promote the use of renewable energy sources. They had already launched a schools initiative called 'Generation Green' and had embarked on an embryonic idea called 'Green Streets': an experiment in how streets can work together to save energy.

We saw the opportunity to transform the Green Streets initiative from eight houses in eight streets into a national movement to reduce the 28 per cent of carbon emissions that come from our homes and make us an energy efficient nation. We also felt that British Gas's 8,000 engineers were a smaller version of the 'salt of the earth' Royal Mail workforce who go out onto our streets and into our homes. We put this to them as 'Bringing warmth to Britain's streets', gas being the warmest and most evocative fuel.

All of this work with corporate allies was promising to bear fruit when disaster struck: in September 2008, Lehmann Brothers went bankrupt and the banking world started to crumble around our ears. Within a few weeks, faced with economic gloom, three of our four potential partners dropped out, leaving only MasterCard saying, 'This is feeling quite lonely. Are you sure you can still pull this off without the funds?'

In a crucial lunch in the City, I asked them to hold their nerve and stick with us. To their eternal credit they did and we managed to get EDF Energy and the Big Lottery Fund to join our band of supporters alongside MasterCard, the Royal Mail, B&Q and the Department for Communities and Local Government. This family of supporters then happily stayed together for a number of years.

Our launch in late March 2009 was a piece of theatre that was exhausting to assemble and an attempt to get into *The Guinness World Records* as well as the nation's consciousness. We built the world's biggest ever invitation in Covent Garden market. The massive temporary work of art extended an invitation to everyone in the UK to come together to have lunch in their streets on Sunday 18 July.

Fittingly, in the old home of London's famous fruit and veg market, the edible 2,000 square foot invite was created using fruit, flowers and vegetables in a single day. This was captured on both stop frame photography and film. The record-breaking design was made up of a staggering 43,000 seasonal ingredients, including 11,000 parsnips, 9,000 cauliflowers and 7,500 apples.

The designer behind the gigantic invitation was Clare Patey, artist and curator of the remarkable Feast on the Bridge, which closes Southwark Bridge to traffic and transforms it into a communal dining space. It feels like a return to medieval or Elizabethan London. Claire was helped by our small, energetic team and by The Big Lunch volunteers from all around the UK, who then went on to host 'Big Lunches' of their own. At the end of the build, the design was carefully dismantled and the produce given away to both passers-by and local charities.

Having hauled thousands of boxes in a human chain, none of us could bear to eat cauliflower cheese for months afterwards. Sadly, the media largely ignored us despite our best efforts. The media talk a good game about supporting good causes but when it comes down to it, if it isn't a humanitarian crisis, a family-based tragedy that writes our domestic fears large or is led by a celebrity, or ideally some devastating cocktail of all these ingredients, then they're not interested. My small and dedicated team who'd been working out of an attic in Soho were very demoralised.

As we moved closer to The Big Lunch itself, however, we did get coverage, notably from the BBC, *The Times* and *Sunday Times* and the *Mirror* group. The BBC interviews included the effervescent Vanessa Phelps, who in a bizarre twist of circumstances, and unbeknown to me, had developed a crush on me at school after my appearance as Lady Penelope from *Thunderbirds* in a balloon debate.

MasterCard also did a charismatic television and print campaign that built awareness. We produced a fun booklet called 'Easy Ways To Serve The Big Lunch' and subtitled 'A Guide to Human Warming'. It contained huge numbers of affordable ideas for street art, music, decorations and growing your own vegetables. Being placed in the cookery section by most bookshops didn't help sales. Being only twenty-four pages, it also had the remarkable knack, which I have personally never mastered, of disappearing when turned sideways.

By the time the day of The Big Lunch dawned we had reasonable awareness and several thousand planned street parties. These ranged from huge events such as a street party in Toxteth for thousands of people from over fifty different nationalities, to modest affairs of several people in a cul-de-sac. We had street parties on bridges, roundabouts, estates (not the aristocratic version!), parks, in private gardens and, logically, in streets.

Downing Street had agreed to stage its own Big Lunch. Unfortunately, Gordon and Sarah Brown couldn't host it and so Alistair and Maggie Darling kindly stepped in. The invitation went to local schools, charities and citizens in Westminster and carried an amusing coda: 'For health and safety reasons, we have decided that guests should not bring their food to share, but, in keeping with the spirit of The Big Lunch, we would like each guest to bring a small token item to raffle for a local charity.'

This surely is the quintessence of Britishness! To be honest, if a rogue homemade sausage roll had poisoned the Chancellor it would probably have delivered us more publicity. I love the restraint, the politeness. I imagined Alistair running the tombola in the rose garden whilst Maggie handed round sandwiches with carefully scripted allergy warnings.

I set off from our own Big Lunch in our street after doing my best to sing tunefully with our street's jazz band (which included a couple of professional musicians way out of my league) and making a quick speech thanking my wife, who had organised it all far better than I ever could.

As I climbed into the taxi and said rather self-consciously, 'Downing Street please', I was in a state of high excitement and anxiety. This was a day on which we had pulled off a national event, against all the odds, at the start of the worst recession in decades. However, it was still too early to really evaluate how successful the day was going to be.

We passed a few London streets having street parties but most were not. My heart sank particularly as we crossed Oxford Street and I graphically realised that for every person participating in a street party there were at least twenty worshipping the God of Shopping. It was ever thus, sadly!

The weather was against us. This meant lots of improvisation and British grit across the various street parties. It also meant that plans to host the Downing Street event in the garden had to be abandoned in favour of the public rooms at the back of the house. Inevitably, this made matters slightly more formal but there was still a happy and bubbly atmosphere.

I enjoyed a good chat with Alistair Darling whom I had never met before but who was, rather like John Major, rather more colourful than the media stereotype. He probably found it a relief to talk about street parties rather than money supply or the 50 per cent tax band he'd just introduced in his second Budget. He seemed genuinely engaged in the cause and I happily updated him.

I then circulated around the room and spotted a couple of teenagers whom I presumed were from a local school or estate. We started chatting and I asked the inevitable question.

'Is this your first time in Downing Street?'

Alistair Darling hosts a Big Lunch at Downing Street in 2009.

They looked at me and then at each other with a rapidly spreading grin. 'No, we live here!'

They were Calum and Anna Darling, Alistair and Maggie's children and residents of No. 11. Children brought up in Downing Street must feel as if they are raised on a film set but they seemed very sanguine about it.

I recovered from my gaffe enough to enjoy the a cappella choir that had been organised to ensure a level of professionalism in the entertainment. As with weddings and awards ceremonies, people are always relieved when they can cease chatting to their neighbour and are able to simply listen. They can also prise themselves away from bores on the pretext of gaining a good vantage point. The choir's gusto and harmony lifted any spirits dampened by the poor weather. Then I made a speech, hoping to build on the good will.

> For many of us there is now no narrative as to why we live where we do, except to earn a wage. Whilst there are a significant minority of communities that are closely knit and act as a beacon for neighbourliness, many of Britain's communities are, at best, anonymous.
>
> According to Census data, 97 per cent of British communities are more fragmented than they were thirty years ago. Millions of people go on social media every day and yet many don't know their neighbours.
>
> We have a record number of people living on their own. We have 5.4 million people working from home, which can be another form of isolation. There are a record number of people on anti-depressants; a record number of alcoholics aged over sixty-five. Tragedies such as the killing of Baby P happen because of the anonymity of our streets.
>
> Surveys all over the world show what our hearts already

tell us: that there is almost a mathematical correlation between happiness and personal security and the numbers of neighbours we know well. We have a phrase for it: Human Warming. That's why we launched The Big Lunch and it has come to fruition today.

Think of summer days as a child when time stopped and friends and family wrapped you in a warm blanket of fun. Add neighbours and you have our picture of what's happening today. In tens of thousands of streets, including Downing Street, people are breaking bread with their neighbours as we speak.

They are discovering that our streets and neighbourhoods are the biggest untapped source of happiness in our lives.

The speech was well received and it was gratifying to have created a homely and uncomplicated atmosphere in a house that was often the polar opposite.

As I returned home exhausted, I felt an enormous sense of pride. We had printed 6 million leaflets; printed and distributed 50,000 booklets packed with ideas; printed our logo on 2 billion letters; been featured in two advertising campaigns.

We had gained the active support of an eclectic group including Baroness Warsi, Nick Clegg, Ed Balls, Boris Johnson, Hugh Fearnley-Whittingstall, Jamie Oliver, Rosie Boycott, Esther Rantzen, Richard Branson, Alan Titchmarsh, Monty Don and Emma Thompson.

That evening, one of our neighbours popped round to the

house. I was up a ladder changing a light bulb and Gaby was sorting out bunting for storage until the next year's party. We're not normally that cosily domestic but it felt like an afterglow.

'I have lived in this street for over thirty years and I just wanted to say that in one day you've changed this street forever,' she said.

Fortunately, many people across the UK felt the same. We asked the Local Government Information Unit to compile an independent audit and report. Some 730,000 people took part in roughly 10,000 events. Parties took place in every kind of neighbourhood from the poorest to the poshest, city and village alike. Thirty-six per cent of participants believed that The Big Lunch brought different ethnic groups together. Eighty-five per cent of people said that their Big Lunch brought people of all generations together.

Thirty-one per cent of participants rated their Big Lunch ten out of ten: 'a complete success'.

Seventy-four per cent rated it between eight and ten with the average score being 8.14. Some 84.3 per cent of respondents felt closer to their neighbours and 87.5 per cent were planning to keep in touch with new neighbours they'd met.

The Big Lunch grew from 730,000 participants in its first year to 2,000,000 in 2011 and a whopping great 8.5 million in the Golden Jubilee year of 2012. The acid test was whether it could continue to be strong post the golden summer of 2012 and it has: 3.65 million in 2013 and 4.8 million in 2014. It thus has an upward momentum and is fixing itself in the national calendar.

The statistics are one thing but the real power lies in what has happened in many communities. For example, Cowgate in Newcastle-upon-Tyne is as tough as the UK gets. The average time from moving into a house in Cowgate and being burgled is twenty-four hours. The few facilities that did exist, such as a boxing club and Scout hut, were bulldozed, leaving a landscape of boredom, even despair.

Yet The Big Lunch encouraged not only a spirit of solidarity amongst the many good people in the community but also some practical improvements. The manager of the middle-class golf course, which had for many years literally turned its back on the community and cursed the stealing of flags, opened up part of their land as a football pitch for Cowgate youth.

This kind of thing has happened all over the UK and it inspired my involvement with the next government.

David Cameron and Nick Clegg host a round-table discussion of the Big Society
in the Cabinet Room just after the first coalition Cabinet meeting.

Chapter 7

Cameron's expensive
dressing gown

D AVID CAMERON PUBLICLY LAUNCHED his and
Steve Hilton's 'Big Society' vision in the Hugo
Young lecture in November 2009 at King's Place.
He overtly contrasted 'Big Government' with 'Big Society' and
proclaimed what *The Guardian* described as a startling para-
dox: 'The recent growth of the state has promoted not social

solidarity but selfishness and individualism.' *The Guardian* noted rather presciently that he seemed to believe that 'solving poverty is a spiritual mission that can be achieved through some sort of collective goodwill' and despite 'an alarming absence of hard cash'.

It was certainly true that social mobility had not increased enough under Blair and Brown, despite rapid progress in their first term. However, it is also true that it was in the Tory-dominated 1980s and '90s that inequality grew dramatically and people learned to let their own financial success insulate them from most forms of social conscience. The atomised and individualised society we often now witness took root under Thatcher.

However, here we had a Tory leader in Cameron at least ready to talk about poverty. Many of us believed in 1997 in the reinvention of the left and the possibility of a 'Third Way' in which the left's social justice could be combined with competent economics. Why not believe in 2009 in the re-invention of the right and the addition of social justice to its often-competent economics?

There is no doubting that Cameron had huge respect for Blair's achievement. As mentioned before, he swiftly stood up as Blair left Parliament for the last time and signalled to his backbenchers to do the same. I am sure he not only admired the consummate skill and smoothness of Blair as a political operator but also his bold land-grab of the middle ground.

The Hugo Young lecture remains the most coherent expression by Cameron and Hilton of their 'Big Society' idea and its breadth and thoughtfulness bear re-examination. Its premise is that up until the late 1960s, the British state had made considerable advances in tackling poverty. This included milestone achievements such as the abolition of slavery, unemployment insurance, the establishment of the NHS and the welfare state, and public housing.

In this historical account, by the way, there is an unfortunate spelling error in the written version of the speech which talks of 'local authorities being charged with clearing *sums*' rather than *slums*. This is particularly ironic given Mr Pickles's later decimation of local authority spending!

Cameron's speech went on to point out that despite a rise in government spending under Labour from 38.2 per cent of GDP in 1997 to over 50 per cent, the fight against poverty and immobility had been increasingly ineffective.

He talked about, by contrast, the 'radical liberalism' tradition in Labour, espoused by Hobson and Hobhouse, which saw the state's role as creating the conditions within which ordinary or poor people can create a good life for themselves. This tradition was presented as almost the role model for the Big Society: self-sufficiency and community action being enabled by a supportive but smart, smaller and agile state.

This idea was contrasted with Fabianism, which says that the state must command and control in order to improve lives. In Cameron's view, this command and control was epitomised by Blair and Brown's obsessive law-making and tax credits. The speech then pointed out that one million 16–24-year-olds were out of work; that the number of people living in severe poverty had risen by 900,000 in the Blair decade and that social mobility had not increased at all in the last thirty years according to the Sutton Trust.

Cameron contrasted the culture of self-improvement, mutuality and responsibility that accompanied the early welfare state with a contemporary benefits system under which teenage mums were rewarded with protection; there were disincentives to work versus continuing on benefits; pensioners who didn't save were given credits, thereby demotivating those who had saved and got no such credits…

'The once natural bonds that existed between people of duty and responsibility have been replaced by the synthetic bonds of the state-regulation and bureaucracy.'

This was a theme later taken up by John Bird, founder of the *Big Issue*, in a very vivid form, in some of our 'Big Society' events. He stated that the guilty middle classes had basically anaesthetised the working classes by doping them with benefits, thereby killing their self-esteem but keeping them quiet.

The Hugo Young lecture went on to lay the foundations of the policies the Tories put forward in the general election: planning rules being put in the hands of local people; new mayors in big cities; devolution of power from national to local level; local authorities listing assets and all local spend; beat meetings where people could challenge the police; directly elected police commissioners and self-governing schools liberated to run their own affairs.

There was much that was coherent and persuasive. There were also some telling weaknesses looking at it now with the benefit of hindsight, that wonderful handmaiden of the sceptic. The speech talked about supporting social entrepreneurs and charities. Yet this support has to include money as a basic ingredient. The severe cuts to the voluntary sector that were subsequently made when Cameron came to power rendered this impossible.

The first time I heard these 'Big Society' thoughts espoused in person was when David Robinson suggested to Nat Wei that we should meet. I first met Nat in the airy but always packed meeting-space on the ground floor of Portcullis House in February 2010.

I was on crutches at the time as I had torn three of my hamstring muscles in an accident the previous December. When I revealed to people that this was due to a water-skiing accident, the sympathy tended to ebb away. Sadly, the pain didn't.

Nat Wei is a fascinating character. He has the smiling, open and trusting face of a child and a super-smart brain. The son of Hong Kong parents, his father was a Chinese pastor – a rarity in and of itself. His parents moved to the UK in the 1970s, and Nat was educated at a tough comprehensive in that glorious global centre of the mini-roundabout, Milton Keynes. (The train smash of a poet and economist's name, both Bedfordshire lads, was an interesting idea for a town's name, but sadly time has somewhat strangled the poetry.)

After Oxford, Nat spent three years at McKinsey, and could presumably have followed a straight and conventional path to wealth and status. Instead, he left management consultancy to help grow Teach First, the innovative scheme whereby the brightest graduates are encouraged to spend the first year or more of their employment teaching in a tough secondary school, usually in the inner cities. When, later, the Big Society started to fail, Nat was criticised for over-claiming his role at Teach First as being that of co-founder. Teach First was in fact founded by Brett Wigdortz. However, Nat also went on to found the Future Leaders Programme, which had similar aims.

Four years earlier, in 2006, Nat had co-founded the Shaft-esbury Partnership, named after Lord Shaftesbury, a Victorian Earl and a contemporary of Dickens who achieved in life what Dickens sought to achieve through his fiction. He tire-lessly supported bills to reduce the number of hours children worked in factories. He helped to transform the way in which people with mental disorders were treated through the so-called Lunacy Laws. He eradicated the use of boys as chimney sweeps and the employment of women and children in mines. He was also an early proponent of the restoration of Jews to their homeland.

A funeral service was held for Shaftesbury in Westminster Abbey, during the early morning of 8 October 1885, and the streets along the route from Grosvenor Square and Westmin-ster Abbey were thronged with 'poor people, costermongers, flower-girls, boot-blacks, crossing-sweepers, factory-hands and similar workers' who waited for hours to see Shaftesbury's coffin as it passed by. Due to his constant work on behalf of the downtrodden, Shaftesbury became known as 'the Poor Man's Earl'. He was a genuinely compassionate Tory. What a shame Mrs Thatcher didn't spend as much time reading Shaftesbury as she did Keynes.

Nat Wei's Shaftesbury Partnership focused on scalable social reforms such as 'The Challenge': a two-month, civic service programme and an initiative to help people successfully transition into retirement.

Nat and I immediately got on. He was an admirer of The Big Lunch, as I was of Teach First and the Shaftesbury initiatives. We had the same kind of overlapping dialogue, cutting off or finishing each other's sentences, as I had experienced with Tim Smit. Little did I know that I was about to swap Tim for Nat. We agreed that I should meet the relevant members of the shadow Cabinet to further discuss my potential involvement in the Big Society.

On my second visit to see Nat, I went to the suite of offices used by the Leader of the Opposition, in the Norman Shaw Buildings next to Portcullis House, the original home of New Scotland Yard. Before meeting Nat, I was attempting to navigate my way into the toilet on crutches when a tall, breezy figure in shirtsleeves nearly bowled me over.

'So sorry. Good Lord, what happened to you?' David Cameron asked.

I explained the rather exotic circumstances of my accident and then, rather than being a nameless member of the temporarily disabled, introduced myself as coming to help Nat with the Big Society.

Our future Prime Minister was just asking me about The Big Lunch when Nat appeared in the same doorway. As we later walked away from Cameron, Nat said, 'Oh, so you two know each other already!' I could have nodded nonchalantly and let it pass into myth but honesty got the better of me.

One of the first people I was lined up to meet was serial entrepreneur, long-time Tory supporter and donor, Martyn Rose. The first thing that struck me about Martyn was his coiffed, bouffant hairstyle, which as a long-suffering, premature baldy I could only admire. The second thing that caught my eye was his bright, yellow socks, which turned out to be something of a trademark. I was used to the interplay of entrepreneurs and strange socks from Richard Branson's tendency to wear odd ones, including the morning we helped launch Virgin Group on the stock market (he claimed he'd dressed in the dark).

I wondered whether Martyn wore yellow as a decoy to suggest he supported the Lib Dems, enabling him to go everywhere as a 'closet Tory'. His cut-glass accent removed the possible success of such a disguise, as did his Trebeck Street penthouse of an office. This was in the midst of Mayfair's elite postcodes, but shadily on the edge of that most upper class of brothel areas, Shepherd's Market. Doubtless a number of well-off shepherds had 'sought some comfort there' as Paul Simon once delicately coined it.

Martyn told me that he had started his working life young, crewing on, and then running, yachts around Majorca. After this Gatsby-like start, from which he still has a perma-tan, he was called to the Bar in his early twenties, but then decided to return to Gatsby and pursue various business interests.

He acquired his first company at the age of twenty-nine and then spent the next three decades developing, refinancing, restructuring and selling a series of businesses. The nature of these companies ranged from publishing software and online academic research to recruitment, soft drinks and commercial radio.

He was a Tory Party donor and close enough to William Hague to attend his birthday parties. He also co-chaired the National Citizen Service with Michael Gove. I found Martyn very personable and he liked my ideas. He was happy to part-fund the setting up of a 'Big Society' organisation that would partner government. He would be chairman and Nat and I would run it day-to-day between us. That was the relatively simple construct put to me, at least until after the general election when the real plot was to be revealed.

So Nat, Martyn and I trundled down the Yellow Sock Road to see Francis Maude and Nick Hurd for what was effectively another job interview. This took place in Francis Maude's significant office overlooking the fast-flowing Thames.

Nick Hurd was the snappily titled shadow Minister for Charity, Social Enterprise and Volunteering. Nick is the son of Douglas Hurd and is the fourth generation of his male family line to be elected to the Commons. Nick has the easy charm of someone who is good looking enough for his son to have modelled for Burberry, and whose family connections mean that, like a Freud, he will always find a place somewhere at the top table.

Francis Maude has the demeanour of someone who's been

around the thrones of power forever. Meeting him was a bit like meeting one of your old schoolteachers unexpectedly in the street: someone from the past you assumed had retired. A one-time criminal barrister, he had first served under Thatcher and Major before spending five years in the City. Maude has the air of a pragmatic patrician. It was difficult even then to assess whether he really felt committed to the Big Society, or simply accepted that as the shadow Minister for the Cabinet Office, he had a responsibility to grin and bear it. Revealingly, he later made the comment that he supports the Big Society but his work as an MP is 'sufficient contribution to it'. No volunteering for Francis it seems!

It was at this meeting that I suggested the idea of breaking tax bills down to their individual, per-household sums, as I had done previously to Gordon Brown. I also talked about getting banks to support charities through their ATM machines, and creating social investment ISAs whereby people could invest some of their savings in social outcomes. Both Hurd and Maude subsequently championed all three ideas without any credit to me as their originator. Such is politics.

They asked me whether I was comfortable working with the Tory Party, aware of my work with Gordon Brown. The decision as to whether to get involved or not was actually one of the most difficult of my professional life but I answered them, somewhat obliquely, by talking about my parents who were 'caring Tories'.

The Big Society was in many ways just a new rendering of ideas put forward by both Blair and Brown: a golden thread of centre-ground political thinking. Iain Duncan Smith's forensic investigation of poorer communities, and his establishment of the Centre for Social Justice, plus Cameron's Hugo Young lecture, persuaded me that there was a depth of knowledge and seriousness in the Tory Party on these issues.

From their point of view, I seemed to pass the test. They wanted to use my experience on Comic Relief, Change the World for a Fiver and The Big Lunch in helping to turn the Big Society ideas into practical, on-the-ground realities. There was just one more 'interview' to go.

I was aware of Steve Hilton from his involvement with the Saatchi & Saatchi advertising campaign for the Tories in 1996. He came up with the 'New Labour, New Danger' poster featuring Tony Blair with demon eyes. Years later, post Iraq, it would have met with widespread support. At the time, although memorable, it smacked of scaremongering, although I did flash back to it when I stared into the real Blair eyes. Steve had also co-founded 'Good Business', a company to promote what became known as Corporate Social Responsibility, with his partner Giles Gibbons, whom I also knew through my charity work.

My first meeting with Steve Hilton was also with Oliver Letwin. Oliver was the quiet, patiently intellectual centre of policy-making, from his book-lined study, whilst Steve was the young radical with the concentration span of a mayfly. It's difficult to describe the churning and disorientating effect of being in Steve's company. He has the defensive confidence of someone below average height. He commands through intellectual bullying. He is like a boxer newly released for the first round. He is also impressively bright and passionate. It's a whirlwind.

I was meeting Steve when his long-standing relationship with David Cameron had entered its closest phase. The friendship had started twenty years earlier, when they were colleagues at Conservative central office. It then blossomed after Cameron's election as party leader when, together, they re-branded the party as green and progressive. Steve was godfather to Cameron's son Ivan and father to his 'Big Society' ideology.

Steve's ideas were already gaining potency and were about to emerge, blinking, into full sunlight. His excitement and nervousness made his manner disturbing and energising in equal measure. I presented him with a short paper which Oliver Letwin leafed through with the measured pace of a tutor and Steve ripped through at an impossible rate.

'This is clearly the brilliant idea,' he said, jabbing a Biro at my notes. 'The mutual. Creating a citizens' mutual. That's very clever.'

I thought so too. I also realised faintly then, but clearly now, that a citizens' mutual, with the ambitions we had, could only be formed by a new brand of politics, of citizen power, that is anti-establishment and therefore anti-Tory: a new political party of democrats.

We shook hands. I agreed to be the CEO of the Big Society Network. I did so on the strict basis that the network would be an independent, challenging partner to government and that it would focus on helping citizens take practical action. The first aspect of this – the independence – turned out to be horribly naïve, which I always feared would be the case.

On taking up the post, I was immediately attacked by a number of friends and colleagues. I had to give up most of my role on The Big Lunch because Tim Smit feared that my prominent involvement in both would politicise street parties.

I passionately disagreed with his decision at the time. After all, he hadn't worried when Gordon Brown's COSA overtly backed The Big Lunch and I then persuaded them to stage a Big Lunch at Downing Street.

The loss of this role was a big sacrifice. The Big Lunch is one of the things I am proudest of setting up and the relationship with Tim has never been the same since. I did, however, continue in a significant but behind-the-scenes role on The Big Lunch 2010.

Nat Wei and I did what you are supposed to do in these situations: we set up a Steering Group. I am not a great lover of committees. One of the marketing directors of Woolworths, in a fit of honesty post its demise, said with a twinkle: 'We faced a crisis and reacted as we always did at Woolworths: we panicked, formed a committee and got overtaken by events.' However, this Big Society committee was thankfully full of doers rather than talkers.

I brought in Kevin Steele who had worked with me on The Big Lunch and was a veteran at organising branded social movements and Oli Barrett whom I knew from COSA. Kevin Steele takes his collapsible bike around London selling and turning ideas such as Climate Week into a reality. He has almost patentable ways of building ideas into movements by making quotes easy for politicians and celebrities to endorse, delivering packages to sponsors and then building systematically from there.

Oli Barrett is impossibly smiley and clean-cut and wears lots of blazers. He magically creates new, bouncy ideas seemingly every other minute. In the social enterprise space, Oli is like a cross between a young Robert Wagner and David Blaine. He started 'Make your Mark for a Tenner', a scheme that challenged over 100,000 school pupils to see what they can achieve in one month, starting with £10. He brought speed networking to the UK and co-founded 'Start-Up Britain' to inspire and help people set up businesses. Exhausted just listening? You should be.

Piotr Brzezinski became my chief operating officer. A fiercely bright Harvard graduate and ex-McKinsey consultant, he had worked at TechnoServe, an international development organisation whose mission was to 'bring business solutions to poverty'. As a consultant in TechnoServe's Ghana office, he helped research, design and execute staple crop and food security projects. Piotr is a thoroughly good man, a workaholic and, as an American of Polish descent, refreshingly classless. In a nutshell, he was a godsend. He later successfully led the campaign against alternative voting.

There were other distinguished folk, but one person amongst our number appeared unannounced and appeared to join the group by some strange osmosis. As a 6 ft 4 man from Belfast with an accent that could give Paisley a run for his money, Steve Moore was not someone who could be smuggled in unnoticed.

Steve's background was unclear at first and frankly remained unclear at last. He had worked for the Tories in the late '80s on employment and welfare initiatives with Lord Young. When I met him, however, he was largely a slick creator of events, having 'curated' over forty conferences on the 'social benefits of technology' including 2gether, Reboot Britain and 2morro.

He was also a strategic advisor to Channel 4, for whom he developed and implemented new approaches to education via the web, games and mobile. He was one the architects of the 4iP investment fund. Steve had written a satirical review called 'Now Before The Weather The War', which with my comedy-writing background should have forged a link between us. Unfortunately, what was later to unfold between us was beyond satire.

I have pushed the term 'portfolio life' to its outer limits, but Steve had more pies than a human has fingers. At first, he also had an incessant desire to lure me to the pub and only gave up in the face of my repeated resistance. Don't get me wrong; I enjoy pubs as much as the next Farage, but I prefer them without strings attached. Steve's career seemed to heavily rely on craic, drink and endless networking. Instinctively, I was suspicious and I was later proved right.

On 31 March 2010, the Big Society was officially launched to the electorate. This was a launch of two halves. The first half was an event by the shadow Cabinet at the Coin Street

Neighbourhood Centre, chosen deliberately as an example of community-led regeneration in south London.

It showcased the Conservative Party manifesto, in every major policy area, with the Big Society as a 'golden thread'. It was a presentation as united and disciplined as anything done by Blair, Brown and Mandelson and organised by Campbell. Yet it has now been forgotten and didn't burn its way sufficiently into the public conscience as the coherent expression of a new kind of relationship between citizen and government. This is partly because New Labour managed to communicate their coherence over a longer period of time running up to the 1997 election and wrapped it all in a description of their new brand rather than a difficult-to-grasp ideology.

Yet despite these flaws, it was an impressive display, let down a little by its rather crass logo of 'Big Society' in yellow with a smiley face in the 'O' and 'Big government' in red with a sour face in the 'O'… and to think that the Tories were espousing adult-to-adult relationships between politicians and citizens! The only thing missing from this logo to complete its fatuousness was a starburst or a large, pointing finger.

George Osborne gave the briefest of intros: a symptom of what was to follow because he has never passed comment in public on the Big Society. However, Phillip Hammond did talk on an Osborne subject: 'Cutting the deficit by building a Big Society'. He spoke of how welfare dependency had cost the UK £350 billion over twelve years; how family breakdown cost £20 billion a year; how 3.7 million anti-social incidents in 2008/09 alone had cost the taxpayer £3.4 billion.

He went on to describe how informal care, provided by families, neighbours and volunteers, saves the NHS £8 billion a year and how tens of thousands of community organisations could be encouraged to step up to the plate and alleviate the state.

He also painted a picture of how self-managing, public sector co-operatives could be created to deliver services efficiently and be partly paid by results. This notion of payment by results subsequently became one of the main reasons why charities and social enterprises were not able to compete successfully for public service contracts. Unlike the Sercos of this world, they do not have the cash flow or reserves or systems to risk payment by results.

Next up was Michael Gove who talked passionately, albeit in his pious, schoolmasterly tone that so often makes one not want to listen. He preached that schools should be engines of social mobility. He talked about the fact that poorer children fall behind progressively at school, from Stage 2 onwards. He cited the fact that of 20,000 pupils who got three As at A level, only 189 were registered for free school meals i.e. officially poor.

He also spoke convincingly of Obama increasing the number of KIPP – Knowledge is Power Program – schools in America, aimed at poorer communities. These had 7.30 a.m. to 5 p.m. and Saturday school days. Indeed, Obama, who had been elected little more than a year previously, was used as a frequent touchstone for these New Tories, just as New Labour had often referenced Clinton. Obama, as we were reminded at this event, had been a community organiser, now a breed to be placed on the highest pedestal by this group of new-think Tories.

Chris Grayling talked about how five separate forms had to be filled out by police for a car stopped with one suspicious driver and four passengers. He also spoke of how the greatest violence occurs in homes with an income of less than £10,000 a year, without appearing to offer any empathy as to why poverty could make you stressed, ergo prone to anger.

Caroline Spelman talked about how 5,000 post offices and 3,500 pubs had closed and libraries were under threat, but how neighbourhood groups could take them over in future, to save them as community assets; the so-called Right to Buy. She also praised the number of local referenda held in Swiss cantons. I think local referenda are a brilliant means of reinvigorating democracy. How sad that they have never happened in the UK since that speech.

Jeremy Hunt spoke of 'collective individualism', which should have been a warning to us all.

Francis Maude suggested the so-called Third Sector should in fact be called the First Sector because it pre-dates both government and business. Good point. He also announced there would be a Big Society Bank to fund voluntary organisations.

Interestingly, Nick Hurd, even though he was shadow Secretary for Charity, did not speak, whereas Nat Wei did. The reason why this happened was only revealed to me after the election. The plan was for Nat to do Hurd's job, but I was not privy to this twist in the plot at that particular point.

The theme of the whole event was clear: 'we'll put you in charge of your own destiny' and the state will often become a tool for citizens.

The second half of the launch involved Nat Wei, David Cameron and I launching the Big Society Network to the good and great at a lunchtime event at the nearby Oxo Tower Wharf.

I was of course nervous and feeling as if I was living in a dream. I remember watching David Cameron, before his speech, very quickly and skilfully pick up the biographies of Nat and I that were in the welcome pack and absorb them. He then played back the key facts from our CVs in his speech as if he had known us both for years.

He talked about us as: 'two of the finest social entrepreneurs in the UK'. It was very flattering and very adroit. He picked up the credentials he had just familiarised and rolled them into a gathering ball of momentum for his big idea. To be fair, he did know Nat quite well by this point but he barely knew me.

In my speech, I wanted to make the Big Society easy to grasp and practical, which remained my ambition throughout my work over the next four years. Here is an extract of how I tried to explain it…

> The Big Society is a society in which we as individuals don't feel small. In a 'Big Society' everyone should feel empowered and supported. Does our society pass this test at the moment? Sadly not!

Individuals and communities have become less trusting, less empowered and increasingly divided:

- Only 31 per cent of people agree 'generally speaking most people can be trusted', almost halving the 56 per cent score of 1959.

- Fewer than two in five members of the public feel able to influence local decisions, a decline of over 10 per cent since 2001, and only 39 per cent were engaged in any kind of civic action in 2007/08.

- Levels of volunteering have remained static since 2001, and fewer than 3 per cent of people go to public meetings.

- Work done on the 2001 Census data, conducted for the BBC, showed that 97 per cent of communities are more fragmented than they were in 1971.

The good news, however, is that we now have more people in our local neighbourhoods with the potential to be change agents. For example, 5.4 million people work partly or wholly from home. There are more and more semi-retired and retired people with a wealth of ideas, a lifetime of wisdom, reasonable health and lots of energy. There are an estimated 600,000 or more community groups in the UK.

How do we encourage more people to pour out onto the streets, from behind our famous twitching curtains, and transform the square miles where we all live?

The first thing we need to do is change attitudes. We have to dispel the idea that you have to be a 'community type of person' or be from a confident, educated background, or have loads of time, to get things changed in your neighbourhood.

We should encourage people to be active in their community because:

- They can make enjoyable use of a passion or talent.

- They can turn a painful life experience they have survived or mastered into transforming, even life-saving, advice to someone else, as a mentor.

- They can reduce their loneliness and increase their self-esteem.

- They understand that taking civic action is practical and saves them money.

Secondly, we should recognise that many people need to start with 'baby steps' and some visceral, uplifting experience of community rather than a disappointing attempt to be worthy. This is why something simple, sociable, enjoyable and activity-based is a better start-point for many people, rather than volunteering to man a help-line, which may be difficult.

We held the first Big Lunch last year, which I spent two years bringing to fruition with Tim Smit and his team at The Eden Project. The idea is simply to get people to sit down and have lunch with their neighbours on a Sunday in July. Some 730,000 people took part in over 8,000 events in every kind of community imaginable. One in three people rated the experience ten out of ten. Many communities have subsequently formed social networking groups and websites. Some are now petitioning their councils and getting things done. People progress.

Thirdly, we need to think about the Big Society from the perspective of different life-stages.

For a young child, the key aspects of the Big Society may focus on mentoring and being mentored in school; or safe, local facilities for sport or play.

For someone who is semi-retired or retired, it might be using their skills to support community charities or lobby local authorities in a rewarding role as 'The Elders' rather than being ignored and palmed off as 'The Elderly'.

Society can only be changed by the aggregation of these individual, local actions that collectively make a national difference. To do this we all need to live more locally and enjoy living more locally. Strong communities taking collective action on energy, transport, crime, growing food, supporting local shops, are the vital missing link in our fight for sustainable resources and happier lives.

We need the rebirth of the milkman and the lollipop lady; the library, the community hall and the post office, and yes, the friendly local pub: the people and places which encourage an exciting sense of collective, local identity and willpower. Then we can make isolation and inactivity history.

We need to give citizens an enormous helping hand in the form of practical advice, resources and incentives. These can only come from a combination of government, business, charities and active citizens. This four-legged approach is what our network is all about.

The Big Society Network is an organisation being set up by frustrated citizens for frustrated citizens, to help everyone achieve change in their local area.

It will be an enormous toolbox of advice, case histories, links to people and resources, using the power of the internet, mobiles and face-to-face action.

We want to increase the proportion of citizens engaged in social action/civil society. We will be helped in this by anger and frustration.

There is a narrow window of opportunity for the anger caused by the recent collapse in trust, for the frustration so many of us feel in being anonymous tax-payers, to be made productive, creative even: to shape a new form of real democracy and energising empowerment.

A real democracy in which, for example, there are video booths in every shopping mall or in Citizens Advice Bureaux for people to spontaneously record their ideas for improving their local area or in which we have a revival of the visceral power of public debates and meetings.

You don't have to feel especially good to join our movement. You just have to be practical.

Reviewing the speech I am still proud of the clear explanation but blanch at the over-ambitious targets, especially with regards to the citizens' mutual. It is a very salutary lesson to ride the exhilarating wave of popular promises, of wild ambition, and then feel its public and humiliating crash as you fail.

At the general election, several weeks after this event, the Tories failed to win an outright majority, which many blamed on Steve Hilton's inability to turn the Big Society into something clear, tangible and believable on the doorstep.

However, courtesy of the coalition, Nick Clegg and David Cameron were soon standing together in the Rose Garden of No. 10, bosom pals, cracking jokes.

A week after the Rose Garden, on 18 May, Nat Wei and I helped to organise a Big Society gathering at No. 10. It was an important, symbolic event: the first meeting to take place, in the Cabinet Room, after the first Cabinet meeting of the first coalition government in the UK since the Second World War. It was, as Will Perrin put it, Clegg and Cameron's first policy outing together.

It was a gorgeous spring day as fresh as the new government. As I strode the familiar road towards the front door, I remembered, with some guilt, that I had last set foot in No. 10 when working with Gordon Brown. It was true that I was pursuing consistent social aims. I was working with the government of the day to get things done. Yet I felt like a hired hand. I was floating like jetsam on some oily tide of political change.

I drew some comfort from the fact that many others that day had committed exactly the same 'crime'. Rob Owen was one of the others who had worked with Gordon Brown. In fact, there were many shades of pragmatism: Geoff Mulgan, who had been head of Blair's strategy unit, was there, as was darling of the left Camila Batmanghelidjh, founder of the now legendary Kids Company. Martha Lane Fox was there in her capacity as champion of digital inclusion, a role also started under the previous regime.

We all gathered in the garden of No. 10, with videos being taken and photographs snapped. When David Cameron appeared, it was as if, in becoming Prime Minister since we last met, he had simply put on the most expensive dressing gown imaginable and found that it fitted perfectly. He wore his new power effortlessly, as if it had always been his destiny.

Perhaps if you're an Old Etonian, with a First from Oxford, who has already spent several years in the limelight, it is an inevitably easy glide into the history books. Nevertheless, Tony Blair looked like an over-excited schoolboy as he entered Downing Street, with several Cheshire Cat smiles going at the same time. David Cameron looked as if he had just won the school debating competition and was going to pick up the cup.

I felt a shiver when David Robinson slipped down the steps last minute into the garden. He and I had chatted in the week prior and I knew he felt it very hard to attend when he was so close to Gordon Brown, who was defeated and demoralised.

When we sat down at the famous extended oval of the Cabinet table, the seating plan was predictable but revealing. I have reproduced it amongst the photographs. Martha Lane Fox and Camila Batmanghelidjh were ranged either side of the PM. Martha was famous and famously progressive and Camila was exotic and bold. This was the money shot for the PM.

Geoff Mulgan and Francis Maude, in turn, flanked Camila and Martha: old hands at politics from both sides of the political spectrum, heavyweight bookends to avoid any sense of sensationalism.

Those of us who had been close to the left – myself, David Robinson, and Neil Jameson of Citizens UK, who had staged the extra leaders' debate at which Gordon Brown was given a standing ovation – were at one end of the table, still on the naughty step.

The PM spoke comfortably and fluently about the tenets of the Big Society and how he wanted it to be his legacy. Nick Clegg then stressed that the Liberal Democrats did not share the same language as the Big Society, but that localism, grassroots action and self-empowerment were all core aspects of liberalism. One could sense already his discomfort at being herded into a Tory agenda or movement, but he nicely balanced separateness with lots of nodding about common values.

Nat and I then spoke. I held aloft a one-hour banknote. Memories of talking about another form of time currency – TimeBank – with Tony Blair, twelve years earlier, in the same room, flashed through my mind. This one-hour banknote, I explained, had been created by a social enterprise called Spice, who were working, with great success, in some of the most deprived ex-mining communities in Wales. They discovered that lots of activities were offered free by the local authorities to the children registered for free school meals. The take-up of these offers was low because they carried the stigma of being 'for the poor kids'.

So Spice persuaded the local authorities to offer these chances to all the children so as to lose that stigma. They then made the children earn these rewards. For every hour they volunteered, they were given a one-hour banknote to spend against rewards such as concerts or rugby matches at Cardiff stadium. It worked brilliantly and the scheme was extended to adults and adult education. To me this was a tangible and creative example of the Big Society in action. It understood how to change behaviour.

The debate that followed was rugged but constructive, with everyone being given a chance to reflect on the Big Society. My notes record that some talked about social enterprises being stuck at a certain stage of development and needing help; of the need to replicate successful social problem-solving ideas across the country. Other people stressed doing, at minimum, three-year programmes not one-year. Everyone agreed that businesses must be involved in a meaningful way rather than asked to pay and then leave.

There were also interesting warnings for Westminster to delegate power but not to abdicate it. There were impassioned pleas to give substantial powers to local mayors. Martha Lane Fox and Will Perrin talked of overlaying 21st-century tools on to eighteenth- and nineteenth-century democratic processes, a theme on which I will elaborate in my last chapter. Community organisers were agreed to be vital. Community engagement, it was stressed by those who knew, must be seen as a vocation.

We left Downing Street buzzing with the electricity of a new era but also starting to grapple the sheer complexity of how to strengthen civic society amidst the worst recession for decades. The headache started before the champagne was even warm.

Martyn Rose, Paul Twivy and David Cameron at a Big Society reception.

Chapter 8

The Chinese lord and the intern with the bare feet

THERE ARE AS MANY secrets in politics as there are in families. Many are lies by omission. One such secret, held back from me, anyway, was that Nat Wei was going to enter the House of Lords if the Tories came to power. This would then enable him to become a Minister for Civil Society, possibly even *the* minister. This would involve him either replacing Nick Hurd or working alongside him. This was, I imagine, pretty unsettling for Nick Hurd (assuming he knew) and it wasn't great for me either.

It had always been billed that Nat and I would be partners in running the Big Society Network. We worked well together. He was more policy-focused and academic in his approach. I counterbalanced with practicality, communication and people skills. To suddenly discover that he was going to be in the government meant I had lost my partner and the Big Society Network had lost its independence.

Nat was elevated to the House of Lords on 3 June 2010, three weeks into the life of the new government. I had not heard the term 'elevated' before – I had used the incorrect term of 'ennobled' and felt suitably gauche. Elevation sounded like some strange form of teleportation used in *Doctor Who*, or something that happened in shopping centres. Each new lord is allowed to invite family and up to four other guests to the ceremony. I was somewhat surprised and flattered to be invited by Nat as one of his friends. The others went back a long way with him: Jeremy Culverhouse and Dominic Llewellyn.

Nat was to become Baron Wei of Shoreditch and jokes started to circulate about there being many barren ways in Shoreditch. Later, the Your Square Mile team and I called our back-up device, known technically as a NAS (Network Attached Storage NAS WEI, extending the use of puns on his name.) He was only the third person of Chinese ethnic origin to become a member of the Lords and the first to be

British-born. At thirty-three, the age at which Christ reputedly died, he was also one of the youngest Lords ever.

As we watched from the gallery, Nat seemed a young and exotic inclusion into this august institution. Feathered gowns were well and truly ruffled. There was much whispering behind hands as he swore his oath. One could almost hear the words 'whippersnapper' drifting skywards. To some, this was one of Cameron's follies. The fact that Earl Strathclyde, the Leader of the House of Lords, had sponsored Nat probably hushed some of the backbiting.

The language of the ceremony was both beautiful and antiquated, with phrases such as 'my lords temporal and spiritual'. Nat's youthful and my balding, 51-year-old, demeanours caused a little bit of confusion afterwards. As we stood in the Prince's Chamber, all nerves gone and much shaking of hands going on, one of the lords came up to me and said a hearty congratulations.

'That's very kind of you,' I said, 'but I think you mean my Chinese friend over there.' I was tempted to say 'my little Chinese friend' but felt it was too Eric Morecambe for the occasion. He moved towards Nat, suitably confused. I wasn't sure whether to feel flattered, or very old and very bald, that I was assumed to be the new lord.

Photographs were taken afterwards in the Robing Room. In the manner of an awkward wedding, none of the friends had talked to Nat's family and so I walked over to congratulate them. They had been very quiet and looked rather uncomfortable.

'You must be very proud of your son,' I said to his parents.

'We are very modest people,' his father said. 'It is not our way to display too much pride.'

'I understand,' I said and felt a quiet respect for their solemn emotion.

When I spoke to Nat's wife about how she felt, she said, 'It's just another boys' club with grand architecture, isn't it? A bit like Oxbridge! I hope it doesn't take him away too much.'

Her honesty was refreshing. Nat and she lived in a council house in Shoreditch. The contrast could hardly be more pronounced or more interesting.

In the months following, I embarked on a dizzying tour of the UK, giving fifty-plus talks and listening to hundreds of charities, community groups and councillors. I realised very early on that to succeed, the Big Society needed to be very practical, very simple and to be backed by tangible investment and action.

It also became rapidly clear that the Big Society suffered from a number of seemingly intractable problems. It was seen as a fig leaf for the shrinking state and the spending cuts; or as a cynical re-packaging of the civic activity that had quietly kept British society intact for hundreds of years. It was party political ergo tribal and divisive.

The further away from London and the south-east one went, the more toxic it became. 'Big' also suggested some seismic change, shifting tectonic plates, beyond the influence of mere individuals: ironic given that it was precisely designed to be about empowering individuals. However, none of this meant that it wasn't right as a vision. It just needed a lot of work.

I was pretty much alone in touring round and listening to people's opinions. Nat did a little bit of speaking at events, but I was pretty much the sole ambassador for most of the UK. Steve Hilton didn't even go round Whitehall departments to evangelise the cause let alone get on a train to leave the capital.

This was beginning to attract criticism, building on the view that Hilton's metropolitan aloofness and new-age mod-ishness hadn't helped make the Big Society an idea easy to grasp by the electorate.

Nat saw Steve Hilton every Friday and reported on our general progress as a network but I hadn't seen Steve for a while. So we arranged an update meeting. I sent him a note ahead of the meeting, telling him what I planned to cover. In addition to seeing many community groups and charities, we were working with McKinsey on a thorough analysis of civic activity and developing a plan for the network.

I was also frantically fundraising and establishing the groundwork for setting up Your Square Mile as a citizens' mutual. We were investigating how we could best support social entrepreneurs and leverage their work; which neigh-bourhoods were interested in taking up new local powers; how we could make participatory budgeting widespread; and new forms of social investment. We had also started to col-laborate with Martha Lane Fox and her 'Race Online' team about encouraging and enabling greater take-up of digital tech-nology amongst people who were unskilled or unconfident.

Steve Moore had hatched a scheme for a Town Hall Tour of ten to fifteen key cities to evangelise 'Big Society' policy ideas and get feedback. My tour of the UK to date had convinced me that Your Square Mile was the way forward. Everywhere I went, people found the Big Society confusing, vague and tribally Tory. Your Square Mile, by contrast, did what it said on the tin: it was about systematically helping people make change in their local community.

My meeting with Steve Hilton was set for 8 July and I wrote both a presentation and an agenda. My fellow attendees were Martyn Rose, Piotr Brzezinski, Steve Moore and Hilton's long-standing friend Giles Gibbons, who was hovering around the edge of the project in an uncertain way. He was later to become a trustee of the Big Society Network.

'Steve doesn't do agendas. He doesn't like PowerPoint either.' This was the advice raised by all of them in a variety of manners: Piotr was practical, Giles was the long-standing friend, Martyn was wise patrician and Steve was the hard-nosed political realist.

They suggested I accept that Steve Hilton would run the meeting, largely without structure, and fire whatever questions he saw fit. I had worked very hard on a thorough and grounded assessment of our situation. I resented the idea that we were simply slaves to one person's whims and insisted on proceeding with an agenda and a presentation. My key points were these:

Ipsos Mori research had shown that six out of seven members of the public had either not heard of the Big Society or didn't understand it. The greatest priority was to create a practical toolkit of 'Big Society' ideas and rights that citizens could use themselves.

Yet 63 per cent of people felt that British society was broken.

We had two powerful catalysts appearing over the horizon: the Queen's Diamond Jubilee and the Olympics in summer 2012. The world's eyes would be on us. What kind of society and country would they see? What kind of society did we want them to see?

There was also a great deal of understandable anger about the recession and the cuts in public services. I believe that anger is a great fuel if channelled correctly and positively. We had a rich civic life and tradition on which to build, including up to a million community groups and a quarter of a million social entrepreneurs.

Based on this analysis, I laid out three goals for the Big Society Network, mainly to be achieved through Your Square Mile.

We met at No. 10. We were ushered into one of the meeting rooms on the ground floor. Steve was late in the time-honoured tradition of proving your own importance by valuing other people's time less than your own. He was agitated.

'So where have we got to?'

'Steve, I've got an agenda here…'

'Forget that, just tell me what you've done.'

'OK, well, as you know, we want to launch Your Square Mile at the event on 13 July with the PM…'

'Just remind me what Your Square Mile is…' (This was wilfully obtuse, as he'd heard it explained a number of times.)

'Well, we're going to set it up as a mutual that anyone over the age of sixteen could join.'

'Why would they want to do that?' (This was the same man who had said that the mutual idea was 'genius' a few months earlier.)

'Because we are going to systematically remove barriers for them by speeding up CRB checks and giving them very cheap public liability insurance. We are also going to give them offers like discounted printing for flyers and posters for events; cheaper gardening kits for community projects.'

The constant rug-pulling went on relentlessly and was not helped by various people around the table doing a complete volte-face on what they had said to me before the meeting. Meetings were ever thus. Tired of their cowardice, I started to point this out.

'That's strange because when we met on Tuesday, you said the exact opposite.'

I was trying hard to maintain my dignity and contain a mounting anger. I had worked night and day both before and after the election; I had lost my role on The Big Lunch and endangered a number of friendships.

The final straw came when I declared that we wanted to pilot Your Square Mile in a cross-section of sixteen tough communities because their need was greatest and it would be an acid test of what the Big Society could achieve.

'Why would we want to do that?'

I rose from the table. 'Steve, from the moment you've entered the room, you have systematically undermined everything I have said. I don't need this. I have worked tirelessly to put your ideas into practice. I am the only person to have gone out on the road and listen to communities and charities who spend their lives tackling this stuff.'

Without waiting for his reply I left the room, noting the dropped mouths at the rebellion against the great, untouchable friend of the Prime Minister. As I rapidly walked towards the famous front door I heard the soft and rapid padding of feet behind me. Steve Hilton rarely wore shoes in Downing Street, an affectation presumably designed to show that the centre of power was his second home. This habit had prompted President Obama to ask, 'Who's the intern with the bare feet?'

'Paul, wait please. I'm sorry. You know that I have always believed in your ideas. The mutual idea is great. Look I'm just very stressed. Come back tomorrow and let's talk everything through. It's a Friday so it'll be quiet. I'll get Annette to fix a time.'

I tried afterwards to work out why his reaction had been so extreme. My pop psychology explanation was that Steve had given birth to this ideology and had reacted irrationally when he saw somebody else holding his child and telling him how it was starting to change, to become unpopular, and it needed to change its behaviour.

The next day, I went back and spent three intense and positive hours with Steve without a single disagreement or interruption. This was fairly remarkable given that most people got twenty minutes with Steve if they were lucky – apart from the man who ran the country, that is.

I am sure that part of the reason he spent so long with me was guilt. Part of it was that he didn't need the terrible newspaper headlines: one of the people leading the Big Society walking out in the early life of the project. Jokes such as 'Does my society look big in this?' were already doing the rounds and there needed to be a strong body of leaders uniting around the cause. Satirist knives were being sharpened; cartoonist's pens were twitching.

Yet the meeting, whatever its genesis, went much deeper than pure pragmatism. Released from the burden of time pressures and other people, Steve and I clicked and overlapped on numerous ideas. I was also able to share my approach to the issues.

We had identified four broad categories of people in relation to civic engagement:

- The 'definitely disengaged or entrenched' who are not interested in civic society or community engagement unless there is a provable, selfish benefit to them, preferably saving them money or giving them a resource. Research put this at ten to fifteen million people.

- The 'emotionally predisposed but not yet active' who believe in the values of community but haven't yet acted on them due to issues of time, resources, confidence or simply not being asked: another fifteen to twenty million people.

- The 'narrowly active' who are involved in their

neighbourhood via one or two passions such as coaching football or neighbourhood watch but who haven't yet blossomed into more rounded community leaders. Around eight to twelve million people.

- The 'social entrepreneurs and natural local leaders' who are already involved and motivated but need more tools, resources and opportunities to expand what they are doing. This group was less than a million people.

My assessment was, and still is, that only a tiny minority of people would go straight from being unengaged to being a social entrepreneur. Most people need to progress up a kind of 'ladder of citizenship' and will settle at their own level.

Steve agreed with this analysis. We also shared a passion for creating tools that would help people to do this, many of them digital and interactive.

For example, many people are tempted to volunteer but think of it as difficult, risking their dignity, and that volunteering is only done by a 'certain kind of worthy person' who is 'better than me' or 'just has more time'.

What doesn't occur to people is that their passion is key to turning someone else's life around: by teaching them a sport or music or drama. It also rarely occurs to them that their difficult life experiences could be essential in helping someone else cope with the same problem.

So I had the idea of developing an online personal planner. By answering ten or so questions about your hobbies, passions, concerns, life experiences, an algorithm would then make some suggestions as to how you personally could start volunteering in a way that was confident, fun and rewarding. We went on to build this planner on the Your Square Mile website.

Steve loved this kind of 'digital does good' idea, as did Rohan Silva, another important and progressive thinker within No. 10. Steve talked about his and Rohan's plan to start a skunkworks within government: to create new digital ways of delivering services and to replace the moribund and expensive way in which government IT needs were met. In fact, on 1 July, the Big Society Network had, with Rohan's support, held a dinner with a host of the 'digirati' as I called them – digital/online innovators – in order to use their skills to help us transform civic engagement.

Steve took me through a large number of his plans and many of them were compelling. Sadly, a number of them have never seen the light of day. There were, however, a number of things that rang alarm bells.

One was over-intellectualisation. He spoke enthusiastically about an event called 'Social Action in a Post-Bureaucratic Age', being organised with Stephan Shakespeare. It sounded fascinating, if a perfect candidate for 'Pseud's Corner', but increased my fear that everything was far too abstract to engage most people: it smacked of 'the clever talking to the clever'.

Steve talked about the new planning ideas whereby local people could develop and sign off a neighbourhood plan, which, if agreed by a majority of local residents, could be used as a framework for fast-track development. It sounded too loose and naïve, too close to a blueprint for developers to print money.

He also told me that Cameron was concerned about the sexualisation of public places and spaces and the effect on the young. Could I please have a think about this? I sympathised entirely with the issue but it started to set parameters for what the Big Society should tackle that were as wide as the M4.

He ended the meeting with a thorough endorsement of what I was trying to achieve and a deal of camaraderie. Just before I left, he said: 'Look, let's try to make these things work over the next year and then we might put you into the House of Lords. You could come and work with us … I won't be there next week but you'll be fine.' He was referring to our imminent launch on 13 July with the PM.

I walked out of No. 10 with his words about 'joining us' ringing in my ears. The motivation was undoubtedly to bring inside the tent someone who could otherwise tear its delicate fabric. My independence was understood and so was its danger. I was alone in the inner sanctum in not being a baptised and committed Tory but I was being offered conversion.

Paul Twivy and David Cameron at the launch of Your Square Mile at Downing Street.

Chapter 9

The birth of Your Square Mile and the death of the Big Society

ON 13 JULY 2010, we launched the Big Society Network at 10 Downing Street. David Cameron was two months into his premiership. It was a boiling hot day and we all longed to be in the garden. For some reason this was not possible. John Bird of *Big Issue* fame showed himself a brilliant opportunist by giving out hand-shaped fans inscribed with the motto of the *Big Issue*: 'A hand-up not a hand-out.' After our speeches I used one of these to cool down the PM, which then encouraged John to make an impromptu speech, as is his wont, holding them aloft.

Some 150 or so of the good and great had gathered, including charity and business leaders, politicians, journalists and broadcasters. The atmosphere was one of escalating excitement, as is so often the case with these events: everyone rises on the thermals of collective self-importance and the possibility of a little bit of history. Each famous face spotted or hand shaken increases everyone's self-esteem by a notch.

A group of us waited for the PM to appear and escort him round the room. As he rose up the stairs, Giles Gibbons said, 'Hello, David', which I felt lacked protocol but reminded me how far back many of these relationships went. Cosy sofa chats between Steve Hilton, his partner Giles and David Cameron, when he first became Leader of the Opposition, floated into my imagination.

Before we knew it, we were into the rugby scrum. Cameras and camera lights were held aloft as jostling people pressed forward to press the flesh of the newly crowned PM. I broke away to make some arrangements around the speeches and returned to the crowd to find Alan Yentob and Peter Fincham nicely bickering.

Alan Yentob is the long-time creative guru and maverick of the BBC and Peter Fincham had left his job as controller of BBC One in late 2007 to subsequently become director of television at ITV. This followed an unfortunate episode in which Peter appeared to suggest that the Queen had stormed out of a photography session during the making of the documentary *A Year with the Queen*.

Alan couldn't resist baiting Peter over his move to the dark side of commercial television.

'Hello, Peter. What are you doing here? I thought you'd given up on anything public service!'

Near them stood David Abraham, chief executive of Channel 4. How ironic to have had these three people in the room, who between them controlled so much of the television output of the UK, and yet never go on to achieve any significant media coverage of our tough ongoing work when it was needed most.

It had been decided that Nat, now Lord, Wei would *not* speak as he was clearly now the government tsar on the Big Society and therefore had to stand apart from the Big Society Network. This soon became an official separation.

Martyn Rose spoke first as chairman of the network and introduced the PM, who started suavely and effortlessly…

'Welcome to my new, modest, Georgian home!'

The room purred with appreciative laughter.

'I am not going to say much. I am here merely as the hors d'oeuvre to Paul Twivy's main course…'

My anxiety rose to the point that I scarcely heard what followed except in its broadest terms. Then it was my turn to stand in front of the famous portrait of Elizabeth I and talk to the modern-day famous in front of me.

Thank you, Prime Minister, and good afternoon everyone. Thank you for coming.

Two out of three adults in this country believe that British society is 'broken'.

The phrase 'Broken Britain' and the idea of a 'social recession' in the UK, as great as the economic recession, create strong and sometimes hysterical reactions. They evoke for many a fear of the anger and unrest that might result from a sharply divided society. For others it speaks of a defeatism they hate. I also hate defeatism.

I want to suggest to you that our societal issues are more complex but also more resolvable than is usually portrayed. Consider this paradox.

On the one hand, we have record levels of social isolation amongst old and young alike, with seven million people living on their own in England and Wales alone. Privacy nurtures but isolation destroys. Ninety-seven per cent of neighbourhoods have become more fragmented since 1971. Average life expectancy varies between the richest and the poorest by fourteen years and the richest 10 per cent of the population are 100 times as wealthy as the poorest 10 per cent.

Our general level of social trust has almost halved since the late 1950s despite the fact that so much else has improved. Sixty-one per cent of us don't feel able to affect local decisions. Only one in thirty-three of us attends public meetings. Only a quarter of us take part in any kind of regular, formal volunteering.

Yet many of us, as disempowered, angry and disenchanted citizens, sit with a 'Berlin Wall' in front of us.

On the other side of this Berlin Wall are an estimated 900,000 to 1,000,000 community groups, one for every six citizens; 238,000 social entrepreneurs, many of them brave, persistent, 1–10-person charities born out of anger and passion, fighting the toughest problems on our doorsteps, only 1 per cent of whom get any kind of formal funding. Imagine if we made it even 3 per cent.

We need to smash down this Berlin Wall so that all of us can firstly see the extraordinary diversity and energy of civic society, of social enterprise and community groups.

We then need to create a brilliant filtering and guiding mechanism by which people can find or create the right groups and enterprises for them, in their local areas, using the starting point of their own needs, issues, talents and passions.

This might then become the Big Society – the solution for 'Broken Britain', which is also, sadly, being treated with hysteria. It has been variously criticised as being a fig leaf for the shrinking state; a PR stunt by the Tories; or, as Ed Miliband described it in *The Observer*, 'an attempt to con progressives … the same old idea of laissez-faire, of self-help, that we saw in the 1980s'.

How do we tackle this hysteria and realise our vision of hope? We need to make the Big Society practical and within reach.

The network will be, with your help, an independently funded and run voice of the citizen, an enabler of the citizen and a challenging partner to government.

We have three goals.

The first goal is to encourage and enable meaningful, local action by citizens, especially amongst those who are currently unengaged.

The second goal is to raise the number of people who take part in groups outside of work and home and to support those groups as they grow. In groups we learn the healthy balance between our own needs and the collective good; real democracy; happiness.

Our third goal is to help community groups and social enterprises to access local powers and rights created by 'Big Society' legislation.

But you cannot herd people into the Big Society like cattle. Anything branded 'Social Re-Engineering: Please Walk This Way' is finished before it's started.

We need to bring people with us in small steps that get larger and more confident with time.

We need to provide tangible rewards and incentives, not just appeal to some vague altruism.

We need to break the UK and the Big Society it needs into bite-sized chunks.

Which brings me on to our first and most important project: Your Square Mile.

There are 93,000 square miles in the UK. We tend to only hear about two of them, the square miles of the City and Westminster, and many of us have felt badly let down by both.

Your Square Mile is about enabling citizens to make changes in as many of the other 92,998 square miles as possible.

Your Square Mile will be a mutual: an organisation owned by its members and run for their benefit.

Every citizen of the UK will be able to join for a very affordable fee of, say, £5 a year, and become a member and shareholder, in receipt of benefits and dividends.

Think of it as a 'Union for Citizens'.

One in three of the UK population are members of a mutual. There are indeed eight million more members of mutuals than listed owners of shares. Every parliamentary group on mutuals has concluded that mutuals are more efficient and deliver better value than plcs. Your Square Mile will be no different.

Maslow famously developed a Hierarchy of Needs.

I would like to introduce a similar principle in relation to citizens: the Ladder of Citizenship.

A small number of people go from being unengaged citizens to tackling an overt problem by setting up an organisation. Thank God they do. For most people, they will start with something much more modest.

They might help a neighbour for the first time. They might help organise or take part in a Big Lunch, as many are about to do this Sunday.

They might use their mobile or a public kiosk to spontaneously register a problem, a saving, an idea and send it to their local authority.

They might join a hobby-based group like Stitch 'n' Bitch or a football club.

From there they might then decide, with that group of neighbours or hobbyists, to save the local post office or start a group for elderly people in a building lent by the local council.

One activity, one baby step, gets people to cross the line from unengaged to engaged.

It is best that we never mention the Big Society but that millions of people cross that line millions of times. Then in three years we will turn round and find ourselves in the Big Society rather than just talking about it.

The speech was very well received but amidst the applause, I noted Cameron's strongly raised eyebrows at my last paragraph. He felt very uncomfortable at the idea that we should let the term 'Big Society' settle into the background whilst we had a few years of quiet but substantial achievement. Whilst politically this was never going to happen, it's probably the wisest thing I ever said on the entire project. The more you bellow from the soapbox before there has been genuine achievement, the more the soapbox disappears into quicksand.

The following Sunday, Tim Smit's nightmare came true. The *Sunday Times* ran a headline saying, 'Come join my street party, says Cameron' conflating The Big Lunch with the Big Society Network. This was because of my involvement with both, and the unfortunate coincidence of 'The Big Lunch 2' with the 'Big Society Network 1'. Tim, however, didn't phone me frothing with rage and two years later, in jubilee year, Cameron staged a widely publicised Big Lunch in Downing Street.

What was revealing and damaging in equal measure was Eric Pickles, who had attended our launch event, saying that his enthusiasm for social action was partly driven by the prospect of cuts of 25 per cent or more in public spending: 'I will confess this is about getting more services for less money.' Cheers, Eric!

On the front page of the same *Sunday Times* was an article about Steve Hilton being fed up with civil service mandarins pushing through policies without consulting No. 10. Thus started one of the battles between 'GOD' and 'Satan', or Gus O'Donnell, head of the civil service, and Steve Hilton, to give them their earthly names.

I embarked on a further series of fascinating discussions and meetings around the UK. One was a two-day visit to Wales. I was invited by Prince Charles's Charities in Wales to talk about the Big Society. Peter Davies, who organised the trip, told me I was the first person connected with government, of any description, who'd felt it important enough to come to Wales to discuss the Big Society; a not dissimilar reaction to the one I had received in Scotland.

Manon Williams, an irrepressible ball of energy and then private secretary to Prince Charles, accompanied me to a dinner at the Prince of Wales's house, Llwynywermod near Myddfai. The countryside was breathtaking and not a drop of rain in the air. We drove up the unmarked gravel track to a police box looking as if it had landed from outer space, and were nodded on to the house itself.

It has the romantic ruins of a former castle or abbey in the grounds. There were probably twenty-five guests – charity leaders and members of the Welsh Assembly – in the medieval-looking dining hall and I was positioned in the middle as the speaker.

When I was presented with the finest lamb the Welsh hills can deliver, I remembered I hadn't told them I was kosher. With many eyes upon me, I wondered whether I could push the lamb around my plate and under my potatoes.

Realising I couldn't, I ate it, praying inside for forgiveness, especially as it was probably the best lamb I have ever tasted!

The discussion was honest and passionate. Many people spoke of the strong tradition of community and mutualism in Wales but also how some of these community bonds were weakening. Generally, there was a lot of suspicion of the Big Society as 'cuts by the side door' but there was also an honest recognition that many Welsh community organisations worked in silos and needed, themselves, to become more interconnected.

The general feeling about civic engagement was that 'we must move the ownership of this to the people of Wales' and a distinctive Welsh narrative was needed to remove the political connotations of the Big Society. In this regard, Your Square Mile was felt to be a strong concept for Wales. This was strengthened by its cultural connotation in the Welsh language: '*Milltir Sgwar*' – 'the place that created you, the location that tugs your heartstrings when *hiraeth* [another uniquely Welsh concept for a yearning that is tied to a particular place] kicks in.'

This experience in Wales confirmed experiences I had

throughout the UK: Your Square Mile was down to earth, truly local and apolitical, whilst the Big Society was vague, top-down and highly political despite intending the opposite. This was a message that I kept trying to communicate to Downing Street, Nick Hurd at the Cabinet Office and the DCLG, as well as within our own network.

It was clear, even at this early stage, that the Big Society Network was never going to be independent from government. It was only going to be allowed to do what Steve Hilton wanted it to do. What did he want it to do? Well, he finally pronounced on this one.

Steve wanted us to stage thought leadership events; find groovy ways of engaging people in social action using digital technology; grab some social entrepreneurs and give them some sort of support whilst laying claim to their intellectual property as that of the Big Society; and give out yet another set of awards. In short, knit some reasonably intelligent fog.

Steve Moore, being a skilled opportunist and fog-knitter, had quickly understood this agenda and started to manoeuvre his way into Hilton's affections as a potential leader.

Moore used to repeatedly say to me in his thick Irish brogue, 'Paul, can I have a word…?' And then, in his mock-elder-statesman-I-am-closer-to-the centre-of-power-than-you manner, continue: 'A bit of advice on how to play this with Downing Street, Paul…'

This usually introduced something he thought was cunning but had 'BEAR TRAP' written all over it. Steve is not the subtlest of creatures.

By October and the first party conference season post the general election, I could tell I was destined for increasing isolation because of my preparedness to tell the truth, both good and bad, and to try to get something of a genuine citizens' movement underway by separating it from party politics. Even if they knew I was right, there was no political glory in any citizen achievements unless they had 'Big Society' branded all over them.

Nat Wei was beginning to hit problems as well. His rapid and odd rise to power would have gone to most people's heads and he became somewhat power-drunk and attached to his own myth. Despite having good intentions, Nat delivered speeches that were too academic and difficult to follow. He started more projects than anyone could count. He asked his alma mater, McKinsey & Co., to deliver what they estimated to be £750,000 of free advice.

He also had the unnerving tendency to approach the same funding bodies that I was approaching – NESTA, Big Lottery Fund, Sainsbury's Family Trusts – and ask for very substantial sums of money for projects that overlapped with mine. This had an unnerving effect on all concerned, including me. I suggested to him more than once that liaison and synergy might not be a bad strategy.

It had become very clear to me that, much as I genuinely agreed with what Steve Hilton had devised in terms of devolution to local level, it was accompanied by record cuts in local government – at 26–28 per cent, the biggest cuts of any area of government – and cuts in government grants to charities which made it near impossible for this much-vaunted localism to take place.

The effect of these cuts became all too apparent when I was invited to speak at a summit of local government leaders on 25 November 2010, convened by the New Local Government Network, or NGLN for short: a group of organisations trying to champion innovation and best practice in local government.

It was clear that many councillors, council leaders and employees felt, understandably, that they had been hit by what I described as a 'perfect storm'. They were subject to the most stringent of all government cuts and those cuts had been made even tougher by being 'front-loaded'.

At the same time, local authorities were being given significant new powers and responsibilities under the decentralisation and localism agendas. Finally, they were being asked to deliver to increasingly empowered, anxious and demanding citizens. No one could deny that this represented a maelstrom of change.

There was a wide spectrum of attitudes amongst councils and councillors about the Big Society agenda. A minority embraced it as an opportunity for radical reinvention in the ways services were delivered or how budgets and priorities could be actively discussed with citizens. Others saw it as taking a cruel axe to front-line services, especially those that protected the most vulnerable. It was sometimes assumed that these negative attitudes were driven by political agendas but they were often more profound and heartfelt than that. There was, however, a resistance in many councillors and council leaders to new ideas and ways of working.

For example, the Networked Neighbourhoods Group had independently produced findings on the impact and popularity of online neighbourhood networks. Fifty-nine per cent of citizens using these networks felt able to influence local decision-making versus a national average of 39 per cent recorded in the latest citizenship survey. Forty-two per cent of users said their attitude towards local councillors had improved as a result of using these websites and 83 per cent of councillors found the sites to be constructive and useful. Yet many councillors had started by viewing these networks with great suspicion. These ideas have yet to be taken up.

Many councillors also viewed participatory budgeting as a threat to their elected status and responsibilities. Yet the evidence, from the 120 or so projects conducted in the UK to that point, was that having vigorous, face-to-face debate with a variety of citizens on budget decisions, whilst difficult, and requiring calm education in the face of partisan causes, delivered the strongest relationships councillors had ever experienced with their constituents. Citizens forced to look at the same difficult choices as councillors became more empathetic, not less.

At the NGLN conference I certainly encountered council leaders hit by the 'perfect storm' and I had greater and greater empathy for them hearing their plight at first hand. I was also struck by how forward-thinking many of them were.

A typical example of this was a remark made in connection with libraries along the following lines:

> I know that if I consult local people about what I should cut first, many people will say libraries. This is because, although a minority of people see them, quite rightly, as essential as any other service and a lifeline to learning, many sadly don't use them at all. What I'd like to do is tell them my view of what libraries can be in the future: not just a place to borrow or read books, essential though that is, but also a centre of online learning, a hub for local discussion groups or start-up businesses.

Many of the people present were the elite of local government leaders, the most progressive, and didn't necessarily represent the average local authority chief executive. Nonetheless, I felt the tragedy of so many inspiring ideas being laid to waste by Mr Pickles and his gang of DCLG cost-cutters. I imagined Pickles, as I often do, at the front of a queue of eager 'schoolboy ministers' saying, 'Please, Mr Cameron. I can cut faster and deeper than he can. Please, sir, let me do it. For the party, sir, for the party!'

It was thus particularly poignant and grievous that it was on the evening of this NGLN conference that I discovered that Steve Moore had shafted me in the most blatant manner possible. We had started to discuss how Steve might take over the Big Society Network whilst I stayed as co-founder and a board director but progressively moved over to running Your Square Mile. When I say 'started', that is exactly what I mean.

Imagine my surprise, then, to be called by a journalist asking me about the change of leadership at the Big Society Network. I enquired about the source of this rumour and was pointed to a blog post that morning at 9.10 a.m. by David Wilcox. David is a social enterprise groupie and relentless blogger who runs a website called Social Reporter. He was also one of Steve Moore's old buddies and Steve had already paid him £8,000 in consultancy fees to create partnerships, blogs and ideas for the Big Society Network. His blog opened as follows:

> I am delighted to see Steve Moore emerge from the confused world of internal 'Big Society' politics as new director of the Big Society Network, with the aim of making it the innovation platform for the UK's Prime Minister's big idea: to build the Big Society.
>
> Steve isn't the man for the formal press release [quite clearly he bloody well wasn't!] and the news emerged via Steve's bio posting to the Athens TEDx event tomorrow where Steve is presenting.

To add insult to injury, Steve had stolen my PowerPoint slides to do 'his' presentation in Athens. Well, if you're going to steal someone's PowerPoint presentation, you might as well steal their job; and if you're going to steal their job, you might as well steal it in public.

I got on the phone to Wilcox and Moore pronto and after

various expletives I won't repeat, I asked them to withdraw the blogs, which they didn't. I then asked Martyn Rose as chairman to see 'fair play', which he sort of attempted in a gruff 'Tory grandee' kind of way.

We finally issued a press release on 2 December:

> Paul Twivy, our co-founder and chief executive of the Big Society Network since February, will become CEO of Your Square Mile and focus his efforts on this major initiative. He will remain a board director and co-founder of BSN and will continue to be involved in the strategic development of 'Your Local Budget' and other selected BSN projects.
>
> Steve Moore, who has been working with the network since the outset, will become its director, running the network over the next several months.

Thus began a separation that had seemed inevitable for a while. Talk of the Big Society failing grew. I set about setting up Your Square Mile and Steve Moore set about doing Mr Hilton's bidding.

They say that success has many fathers but failure has a few select scapegoats, as I was to discover one Monday morning on the front page of *The Times*. The article was written by Sam Coates, the deputy political editor, and appeared on 24 January 2011. It stated: 'Steve Hilton, the Prime Minister's director of strategy, has privately made clear his worries that the "Big Society" message is being drowned out by Labour and cash-starved charities that are defining his project in a negative light.'

There were a number of interesting, not to say ludicrous, aspects to this sentence. Firstly, the ironic use of the word 'privately': so 'private' indeed were Hilton's comments that they appeared on the front page of a national newspaper. How convenient for him that a right-wing paper happened to overhear his private scapegoating!

The second absurdity was the idea that an ideology, such as the Big Society, could be defined by its detractors. Surely this suggests that the ideology in question must be largely hollow in the first place. Thirdly, there was an accusation that charities, as some of them tumbled over the cliff of insolvency, were wilfully attacking the Big Society as an act of spite. In fact, ACEVO estimated that charities would be losing £4.5 billion of funding in the forthcoming year from government cuts and, as Terry Stokes of Lasa was quoted saying later in the article: 'If you cut the charities, you are cutting our ability to help each other, you are cutting what structures our neighbourliness. This is what the Big Society is all about, so you are pulling the rug from under that.'

The article went on to describe 'crisis talks' between Steve Hilton and Phillip Blond. Phillip is the founder of think tank Respublica, author of 'Red Tory' and stepfather of the Big Society.

Phillip is a curious mixture of academic, political philosopher and theologian. He is bright, garrulous, sometimes pretentious but never dull. He appears to have walked out straight of an eighteenth-century coffee-house elite. His intellectual spikiness reminded me of Stephen Bayley, design critic and self-described 'second most intelligent man in Britain', with whom I had some strange dealings over the Millennium Dome.

Phillip Blond could be incredibly supportive both of Your Square Mile and of me personally. He used to frequently say, 'You actually get the idea of a civic economy, Paul, which most of these buggers don't.'

Phillip was weighed by the Tories and found to be an asset and a liability in equal measure. He was always great on *Newsnight* for a bit of intellectual credibility, but could misbehave in public. He did have the guts, however, to correctly point out that there was a substantial body of policy underlying the Big Society. He was prepared to stand up and be counted for the ideology he part-founded, which very few politicians were. Sadly, they went on to dump him, as they did with so many of the people trying to make their ideas work.

The Times suggested that Mr Hilton and Mr Blond 'harbour concerns about the performance of Lord Wei, the Tory peer brought in to explain the agenda to the wider public, and Paul Twivy, chief executive of the Big Society Network. A national "Big Society" roadshow last autumn was cancelled after there was heckling at the first event in Stockport and the mood turned ugly.'

It neglected to mention that I wasn't CEO of the Big Society Network any more and hadn't been for two months. More importantly, it neglected to say that I had nothing to do with the ill-fated event in Stockport which had been hastily and badly conceived by Steve Moore and then very badly facilitated by him.

It was very clear that Nat and I were being used as public fall guys. It is difficult to express how angry I felt. I had been the one person to go out on the road, listen, learn and construct a tangible and systematic means of trying to help people strengthen their community against an ever-worsening economic outlook under the banner of making the Big Society work. I only decided it had to be done under another banner when the Big Society had become too toxic to handle.

The day after the *Times* article appeared, I spoke at a conference organised by the NCVO, the umbrella organisation for UK charities. It was a conference about how to campaign successfully for social causes. I was on a panel that followed an address by John Bercow, Speaker of the House of Commons, who gave some useful tips about how to navigate Westminster and its processes.

I talked firstly about The Big Lunch as an example of fighting against the odds to get something national started. I then went on to defend the Big Society as being founded on a wide range of policies, but also acknowledged its problems and lack of popularity. Finally, I talked about how I hoped Your Square Mile could succeed by being apolitical and led by local people, with us supporting as a background enabler.

In the Q&A afterwards, I was asked how I could possibly

still defend the Big Society in the face of its obvious cyni-cism and the government cuts. I answered by saying that, like many ideologies promoted by a Prime Minister, the Big Society was divisive even within the Cabinet, just as Blair's 'Third Way' had been. I also said that it was unpopular with many members of the public.

Later that day, a fairly inexperienced journalist called Kaye Wiggins from *Third Sector* magazine put an article online with the headline 'Big Society idea "divides the Cabinet" and is loathed by the public'.

To this day, I don't believe I use the word 'loathed' but no one filmed the panel or audio-recorded it and so it can't be proved conclusively either way. Whilst writing this chapter, however, by the miracle that is internet search, I have found record of a series of Twitter feeds made by the self-styled 'hackofalltrades', who reported my speech as it happened.

In the tweet timed 11.12, he reported me saying:

> Twivy: what is Big Society? PM pushes it, most of the public don't like it or don't know about it, but a few of us think it can work.

Please note the moderation of my directly reported language and my continued support for the idea.

I took Kaye Wiggins to task and was given due right of reply about being quoted out of context in an article. All fell quiet, or so I thought...

A fortnight later I was driving to Gorleston in Norfolk,

with my trusty sidekick Olivier Severs, on the way to the first of our Your Square Mile workshops in the sixteen areas we had chosen for pilots. More of this anon. My mobile rang. It was my son.

'Dad, it's Max. My friend has just heard you quoted on Prime Minister's Questions.'

'Really, in what context?'

'Apparently Ed Miliband quoted you as an advisor to Cameron who has said that the Big Society is increasingly loathed by the public.'

I felt the temperature in the car plummeting to sub-Arctic and it wasn't the brisk Norfolk air coming in through the blowers.

I finally got to see the BBC Parliament recording of PMQs the next day.

I was in good and passionate company that day. Miliband also quoted the CEO of Community Service Volunteers saying that government policies are 'destroying the volunteer army'.

He went on to quote that billions of pounds were being cut in the charity sector and that the Daycare Trust had said that 270 Sure Start schemes were likely to close. The LGA had also said that Eric Pickles was 'detached from reality' in thinking that vicious local government cuts wouldn't affect front-line services. So my 'quote' was simply the last of a series of well-aimed missiles.

Miliband was at his hectoring best and passionately attacking the cuts to charities, Sure Start centres, libraries and community centres. Cameron put a pamphlet in the middle of his notebook as he sat down before the next question. It was clear he was getting ready for something he knew was coming down the tracks.

'…and if the Big Society is so successful, then why has the Prime Minister's own advisor, Paul Twivy, said that it is increasingly loathed by the public?!'

The PM angrily threw his notes on to the despatch box, which got a whoop of 'temper, temper' cat-calls from the opposition benches. I am sure that had I been present he would happily have throttled me.

He then retorted with the mock pamphlet he'd already prepared for the cause: 'one I prepared earlier', to use the *Blue Peter* parlance. It said 'My Fresh Ideas' on the front cover plus a mock Labour logo, although, rather oddly, and with a distinct lack of attention to detail, it was printed in light Cambridge blue not Labour red.

'Labour have published their fresh new ideas,' the PM said, as confidently as he could. 'The tree was chopped down and … [he flicked through it with a self-satisfied grin to show empty pages] … there is absolutely nothing in it.'

Cameron went on to challenge Miliband to support the Big Society rather than attack it. Interestingly, Clegg, clearly in view sitting next to Cameron, did not look impressed by the PM's responses.

Miliband came back with more, including a stinging observation by David Davies, a Tory MP: 'If you talk about a small state then you sound like Attila the Hun, but if you talk about the Big Society, people might think you're Mother Teresa.'

Miliband then says of Cameron: 'I have to say that after what he's doing to charities up and down this country, nobody is going to believe that he's Mother Teresa.'

Cameron then retorts that the cuts are only necessary because of Labour's mishandling of the economy.

The battle was raw, passionate and full of polished, political prize-fighting. It was also profoundly depressing.

I agreed with Miliband that the means of achieving the Big Society were being cut at alarming speed. I also agreed with Cameron that unity in tackling tough societal challenges was both necessary and desirable.

However, Cameron had not created an atmosphere within which the societal crisis could be dealt with like a war. He had instead created a Tory brand – the Big Society – behind which no Labour leader, no charity leader and very few citizens were going to rally. The deeply ingrained habits of the old left–right blame game won the day yet again.

I wrote to the Prime Minister explaining the true context of my remarks, which was politely but coldly acknowledged. I also wrote a letter, which I offered for publication to *The Times* and *The Guardian*, who both ignored it, which was finally printed in the *Telegraph*.

In the letter I pointed out that 'to acknowledge that many members of the public dislike or mistrust the Big Society is not to oppose the concept; it is merely to confront its challenges'.

I went on to point out that:

The prerequisites for making the Big Society work are

mainly practical. We need to remove the barriers to volunteering by making CRB checks simpler and more portable between charities; provide affordable public liability insurance for all community activities; and explain to everyone how the politics of their neighbourhood works and their new rights under localism legislation.

Before my letter was printed (not that its appearance would have made any difference), I received a phone call from Steve Hilton.

'Paul, it's Steve. I need to be absolutely clear that you are never to speak about the Big Society again in public. Do you understand me?'

'Steve, I find it extraordinary that you don't understand the context within which my remarks were made and how a political researcher has found something in *Third Sector* magazine which has been misquoted and already corrected by me. It was just fed into Miliband as political fodder for PMQs.'

'I have spoken to people who were at the NCVO event and they say you were critical of the Big Society.'

'Then they are clearly not reporting all the comments I made in support of it and the passion with which I also defended it.'

'Paul, you are not to speak about the Big Society again in public.'

'Steve, I will not be gagged, not by you, not by anybody. I will stand up for what I think is right.'

A few weeks later, David Cameron held a private dinner

at Downing Street to thank those who had helped with the Big Society. I overheard Steve Moore and Martyn Rose brag about being invited. Nat Wei and I were not on the guest list despite having done more than anyone else to make the cause work.

On Valentine's Day 2011, Cameron wrote another love poem for the Big Society at Somerset House. It was in front of an oval-shaped audience of a couple of hundred people: friends and sceptics alike. It was one of those 'down to shirt sleeves' events.

Two things became very apparent to me. Firstly, that Cameron has a very strong sense of civic duty. His tenacity in presenting and re-presenting his idea in the face of continued cynicism and hostility was testament to that. Secondly, I saw that this drive within him is trapped within a narrow experience of the world. I don't mean a world as narrow as Eton or Oxford or the Westminster elite.

He spoke about people in his Oxford constituencies working together to save public amenities such as swimming pools, tennis courts and pubs as an example of the Big Society at work. These constituencies were, and remain, largely affluent and genteel. This is the world of village fetes, tombolas and car boot sales. It is a world I know very well because it is the world my parents often inhabited and therefore I experienced and absorbed as a child. It is full of sincerity and good people but often ignorant, except in notional terms, of the grinding poverty that exists not far away.

Between February and September of 2011, Your Square Mile

worked in sixteen communities. These communities brought that grinding poverty, and other intractable problems, sharply within my understanding and they changed my life.

To achieve a 'Big Society' or Labour's 'good society', we need to start with 'local society': encouraging and enabling people to make change in their neighbourhood.

Paul Hawken in his book *Blessed Unrest* estimates that there are at least a million organisations working towards sustainability and social justice, many of them very local in nature. He calls it the largest social movement in history. As Margaret Read said: 'Never doubt that a small group of thoughtful citizens can change the world. Indeed, it is the only thing that ever has.'

We chose the communities in conjunction with our funders: the Big Lottery Fund, the Barrow Cadbury Trust, the Calouste Gulbenkian Foundation, the Asda Foundation and Malcolm Offord. Malcolm is the only private individual to have backed us and did so out of a passion to help some of the poorer Scottish communities. A very successful City fund manager, Malcolm was born in Greenock and he supported our pilot there and in Pollokshields in Glasgow.

He describes himself as 'the only Scottish Tory left' and, interestingly, has recently campaigned for the kind of English devolution that was a founding principle of Your Square Mile. He believes that Manchester and Birmingham should now demand their own settlement: 'The industrial working classes should say to the Scots, thank you for agitating on our behalf, we don't want to be bullied by Westminster either.'

Our sixteen communities were from all four countries in the United Kingdom. They were deliberately chosen to be a mixture of urban and small town/rural. We had two ex-mining communities: Manton on the edge of Worksop in the Midlands and Glyncoch in Wales.

We also had small towns with big issues. One was Wigton in Cumbria, which had the first youth curfew anywhere in England. Another was Gorleston, to the south of, and adjoining, Great Yarmouth: a coastal town that had lost most of its industry; open to the world from the sea, but almost closed to England by inadequate roads.

We went to tough inner-city communities, some well known such as Toxteth and others less well known such as Northfield in Birmingham and St John's near Lewisham in south London (where everyone was near-silent with depression).

We had two pairs of communities that were next door to each other to see if, and how, we could encourage adjoining neighbourhoods to help or learn from each other. This included Hoxton and Shoreditch, who had rival gangs and other turf wars: for example Hoxton clubbers parking in Shoreditch and disturbing the peace in the silver-grey dawn hours.

The communities also included Caw and Galliagh, which had experienced much more serious turf wars. They were a Protestant and Catholic community, cheek by jowl in the city with two names: 'Londonderry' favoured by Union-ists (renamed in recognition of its connections with City of

London livery companies during the Plantation of Ulster in the 1600s) and 'Derry' favoured by Nationalists.

When you average it out across the sixteen areas, 27 per cent of the population were in lower-income households and 40 per cent lived in social housing. In seven of the areas, 70 per cent of the entire population were in the highest band of multiple deprivation. If our ideas could work in these areas, they could work anywhere.

We systematically approached these neighbourhoods with the same forensic but supportive approach that the Centre for Social Justice had taken. We pounded the streets; read and talked to the local media; met with local community groups, charities, teachers, the police and councillors.

We found local leaders: people who inspired a widespread body of support and trust and transcended party politics. We then asked them to be our local chair and to run the pilots. They would lead with our support and the support of local project leaders.

We then set up workshops composed of twenty to thirty already active citizens and forty to fifty people who were totally unengaged. The latter were very diverse in age, from sixteen to eighty-five, and in ethnic and educational backgrounds. We recruited them from the darker corners of the communities to ensure that new and ignored voices were heard.

In these public workshops, working with Ipsos Mori, we systematically stimulated, supported and listened, listened, listened. We looked at the likes, dislikes and needs of the area; we physically pinned all the assets of the area, from lollipop ladies to parks to charities, onto maps, the riches of which never ceased to amaze the residents. They were unaware of how much was on their doorstep.

We explained their citizen rights under existing and new localism legislation; we showed them inspiring examples of other communities turning themselves around. We then asked them to generate projects, shortlist and present them and vote on them as a group of seventy. Local leaders were then asked to step forward to run each project.

As a result, we generated ninety projects – five in each area – and gave the community a local website populated with their ideas and a video of the highlights of their workshop. We helped the local leaders with their action plans and connected them to funders and other resources.

All of these workshops and pilots were memorable, but some were especially so.

When we arrived in Pollokshields in Glasgow, we found it very difficult to locate the Nan Mackay community centre, where the workshop was due to take place. This was partly because it was ringed by streets of millionaires' houses, which made us feel we must be in the wrong place.

Yet, no, this was just one of the most extreme examples of the rich living cheek by jowl with poverty and ignoring it. Most poor areas of the UK are not clearly flagged by huge, decrepit tower blocks or sink estates. Poverty is much more subtly and pervasively present on our landscape than that.

The second reason we found the Nan Mackay Memorial Hall difficult to find is that we expected it to be modest, but not a fifty-year-old Portakabin with a leaking roof. It was not identifiable until the unforgettably warm and irreverent figure of Bill Lawns emerged from it dressed in an electric-blue top. Bill started one of 125 community projects in Glasgow in 1982 and his is the only one to have survived, which tells you something about his tenacity.

The Nan Mackay Memorial Hall acts as a lending library, and organises outings, holidays and theatre trips for those who couldn't otherwise afford them. It does traditional craft classes and far-from-traditional digital skills classes. It offers a free monthly hearing check, yearly eye check and mobile chiropody. It hosts tai chi, indoor bowls, healthy cooking classes and a lot more besides. Much of their work is with older people, but people aged nine to ninety cross their threshold most weeks.

All of this is managed on shoestring budgets. Bill says he has the best job in the world despite the ever-present financial threats and his long commute to and from work from his home in the Highlands. This country couldn't function without people like Bill Lawns and his community centre of glowing warmth.

I invited Bill to speak about his work on a number of occasions, most memorably in April 2012 to a round-table group of charity CEOs organised by Sir Stephen Bubb of ACEVO. We were in the beautiful Victorian dining room of Farrer & Co., distinguished lawyers. In fact, it was the very room in which Charles Dickens signed his will, overlooking Lincoln's Inn Fields.

Bill had a way of taking down the barriers on these rather formal occasions. He spoke directly and without sentiment about the needs of the residents of Pollokshields, largely unhelped by the millionaires that surround them.

> I can tell that you are all people of good heart. I meet lots of people and I can usually get a strong sense of them straight away. I sense this is a room full of big hearts and I am telling you that things need to change for local charities like mine, or we won't survive. Please help me, not with money, but with advice and influence. We never, ever give up.

I looked round the table and there was not a single dry eye. The spirit of Charles Dickens, the social reformer and champion of the poor, was still very much alive in that room. I am glad to say that Bill is now progressing his plans to rebuild his community centre, with his Big Lottery application looking positive.

I also remember turning up at the train station in Retford, north Nottinghamshire, and saying, 'Manton, please' to the taxi driver, only for him to reply, 'Cash only for Manton, mate.' He explained this was due to the number of people who ran off without paying.

Manton's main source of employment for 100 years was Manton Colliery, sunk by the Wigan Coal and Iron Company in the late nineteenth century. The village was constructed soon afterwards to accommodate the families of miners who came from many parts of the country to secure employment.

Two miners from Manton Colliery made headlines in 1984 by challenging the miners' strike's legitimacy under the NUM's constitution, and winning a verdict that the strike was illegal. The Manton miners voted overwhelmingly against the NUM strike in 1984. Their pit was finally closed ten years later and some seventeen years before we arrived. Nothing had replaced it as a major employer in that time. There were two generations of unemployed people in many families.

Yet we arrived in Manton to find a community that was the absolute epitome of what the principles of the Big Society could achieve without ever being called the Big Society.

Under Labour, Manton Community Alliance was sponsored by the DCLG for seven years from its inception. The alliance believed that the old ways of 'neighbourhood renewal' were not sustainable. In 2004 it developed its own social capital model and adopted 'residents are part of the solution rather than passive consumers of public services' as its ethic.

Gone was the top-down, short-term project approach to tackling local problems, replaced by the belief that sustainable change comes from a new relationship between residents and the public sector. This new relationship was all about common aims, mutual responsibility and the collaborative action of residents, councillors and the public sector working as equals.

Manton Community Alliance had been an innovator: researching, testing and delivering different tools, many new to the UK, designed to give local people more influence over the services they received.

The results spoke for themselves:

- Sixty-two per cent of the population was participating in the community.

- Forty-one per cent of residents believed they influenced what was going on in their community; 11 per cent higher than the national level.

- Twenty-five per cent of the population voted in a participatory budgeting programme to decide local spending priorities. Many of these people had never voted in an election before.

- For the past three years, crime levels had been tumbling.

- Public spaces were being brought back into use.

The scale of their achievements humbled us, as we were humbled by many of the people we met throughout the UK who made community improvement their vocation; and it *is* a vocation, as the very wise and committed Neil Jameson of Citizens UK has pointed out.

Manton Community Alliance's achievements should have been trumpeted from the hilltops by the coalition, even though they weren't responsible for any of them. They should have been studied for replication. We invited Richard Edwards, who led the alliance, to our national launch to showcase his achievements and to meet Nick Hurd, Minister for Civil Society, and Tessa Jowell. We promoted his ideas to both the Cabinet Office/the Office for Civil Society and to the DCLG as a model with provable results.

The alliance's funding stream was coming to an end in December 2011. We lobbied for them to continue to be funded, both for their own community's sake and also to enable them to teach successful models to other struggling communities. I made personal and persistent contact with Nick Hurd and Greg Clark, the Minister at the DCLG. A DCLG representative was sent to meet them. They were turned down for funding by both government departments. Not a single pound was forthcoming.

This is when I lost all hope of the government supporting the people who turned their vision into a reality on the ground.

Other memorable workshops included arriving in Glyncoch, to beautiful Welsh countryside, but the less than gorgeous Nissen hut, with its corrugated iron roof, that the residents were forced to use as their community centre. Glyncoch was ravaged with problems.

There was, for example, a newsagent and off-licence that persistently sold cheap alcohol to kids as young as thirteen or fourteen. It was so well known that teenagers from all the nearby villages or towns also came visiting, with the consequent problems you can imagine. An enterprising group had designed willow sculptures for the Glyncoch community garden and walks near the town. The drunken teenagers just set fire to them.

Yet we had the most wonderful warmth and incredible response to our workshop and subsequent ideas. We successfully helped them in a seven-year battle to build a community centre by raising the final £40,000 of the £793,000 needed. By providing everything from training to health and social services, this centre has started to turn around the community.

As we saw earlier, Wigton in Cumbria was the first town in England to have a youth curfew due to anti-social behaviour. It is a small town with limited job opportunities and poor transport links. One of the projects put forward in our workshop was by Sam Massey, a member of the Wigton Youth Association, which had been running for eleven years. The idea was to stage a youth festival, designed and organised by teenagers themselves, to which the whole town would be invited.

They embarked on their project but found the going tough, with the mayor initially telling them they couldn't do it. This made them more determined, not less. We managed to get them a grant from O2's 'Think Big' programme and they designed an excellent festival called Something For The Summer. It has now taken place three times in the last four years and with increasing success. One of Wigton Youth Station's projects earlier this year has cut youth crime in half.

Our toughest brief was Toxteth/L8 in Liverpool. Liverpool had been chosen to be one of four 'vanguard areas' to pilot

'Big Society' ideas. Cameron launched this vanguard idea in Liverpool in July 2010. The *Brookside* and *Hollyoaks* creator, Phil Redmond, had agreed to lead the pilot. It looked an unlikely combination and proved to be so. In February 2011, Liverpool City Council threw down the gauntlet, refusing to take part in the pilot. Council leader Joe Anderson said, 'I'm not prepared to try and pretend the Big Society is going to deliver.'

This was the backdrop to our workshop in Toxteth. In the week before, tweets were warning us to 'strap our body armour on'. We were met by the likeably mischievous Tommy Calderbank. Tom had the best job title I have ever encountered: 'director of curiosity' for a charity called Bearhunt. Tom was our local chairperson.

The atmosphere was electrifying and tense. Tom gave a brilliant intro. He started with playing a word association game with 'Toxteth', to which everyone replied 'Riot'. He then went on to systematically dispel the myths about Toxteth.

Toxteth is over 1,000 years old and is mentioned in the Domesday Book. For many years it comprised two aristocratic manors and then royal parkland with brooks, creeks and a waterfall. Puritan farmers took it over and it established a famous pottery.

In the eighteenth and nineteenth centuries, the ancient parkland of Toxteth was urbanised by the wealthy merchants of Liverpool, and huge Georgian and Victorian houses were built along Prince's Road/Avenue boulevard.

Famous Toxteth residents have ranged from Jeremiah

Horrocks, the astronomer who first proved that the moon moved in an elliptical orbit and predicted the transit of Venus, to inventive Victorian merchants, to Margaret Simey, famous campaigner for the poor, to Ringo Starr, whom Tom described as 'the best Beatle'.

This was a brilliant example of how a neighbourhood, by grasping how dynamically it has changed through time, can also see how it could change in the near future and shake off any stereotypes: history as liberation.

After Tom's intro, it was my turn to speak. I told everyone that Your Square Mile was a social enterprise; that we had no affiliations with any political parties, nor had we taken a single pound of government money; that we were funded by foundations and that we were there to help them but always by working with, and through, local leaders.

There followed a barrage of questions:

'Did you come first class on the train?'

'Why, when I Google your name, does the Big Society come up?'

'Why have you chosen Toxteth? Why not other areas?'

'What about the cuts?'

'Have you got money to give us for projects?'

I answered all the questions as straightforwardly and honestly as possible and gradually the hostility dropped from red level 'They're Tory scum in disguise' to orange level 'They might be OK or they might be scum, but we'll give them an hour or so.'

After everyone had started their first discussion at the tables, a man came up to me and said, 'Well done on being honest. If you had started spouting the Big Society, I, for one, would have knocked your block off.' He was a vicar.

The workshop turned into the most vibrant we had and some very strong projects emerged. Sadly, most of them withered on the vine but we did manage one success.

Tiber is an organisation that is working to develop a 5.5-acre piece of land into community arts, sports and education facilities, on Lodge Lane, in the heart of Toxteth.

Tiber involves 14–18-year-olds in every step of this process and encourages them to become positive role models in and around the Liverpool 8 area. The young people are offered training opportunities, involvement in entrepreneurial projects, enterprise and leadership programmes. We gave £1,000 to Tiber, which enabled it to survive long enough to go on and win a £100,000 Mary Portas grant.

If you ever want cheering up about the spirit of the UK, you need to look at the sixteen short films we made about these workshops in 2011. Or look at our documentary on five of the projects. They are on YouTube. The energy and tenacity of people in these very tough neighbourhoods was and is remarkable.

It was in these modest community centres, with their spirit of collective problem-solving, not in the grand and hallowed rooms of Downing Street, that I found reasons to believe in a bright and humane future for the UK.

Whilst we were working with our sixteen communities and building our website, the politics grew ever more difficult between the Big Society Network and Your Square Mile, and we agreed to separate completely.

Martyn Rose agreed to resign as a chairman and director of Your Square Mile and I as a director of the Big Society Network from 31 May 2011. The Big Lottery grant was transferred from Big Society Network to Your Square Mile and we moved into our own offices in Clerkenwell. Sharing an attic office in Somerset House had proved to be increasingly claustrophobic.

On 27 April Martyn Rose, Steve Moore and I met to sign the paperwork. The Big Society Network owed me some salary for my work on participatory budgeting and other tasks. After Steve had departed, Martyn made me an offer.

'We could pay you the money as if it were buying some intellectual property from you. That way you needn't pay income tax and NI on what's owed to you.'

'No thanks, Martyn. I want to be paid through PAYE and pay my tax.'

'You're the first person I have met who is happy to pay their full tax, but fine.'

Never trust a man who wears yellow socks!

Nat Wei had been dropped like a stone. Not only had the original, ill-conceived plan of making him a minister not happened, but also he had never been paid for his work at the Office for Civil Society. Worst of all, he had been turned into a whipping boy for all 'Big Society' failure. In February he had announced that he was reducing his commitment on the Big Society to two days a week.

On 24 May, Nat publicly announced his resignation. The Big Society tsar had gone the way of many tsars and been assassinated. Cameron made some platitudinous remark and Nat vanished from public life.

A month or so later, I went to visit Nat in the House of Lords. It was a beautiful summer's day and we found a quiet corner in the gorgeousness of Victorian Gothic, Pugin wallpaper and octagonal tables that is the Royal Gallery.

We shared stories of disillusionment and cast a nostalgic eye back to the heady and naïve pre-election days of promise and excitement. I felt for his pain and isolation in this lofty and grand place. Yet he was far from despondent. Indeed, he had an air of serenity that perhaps befits a pastor's son.

He talked about how short a period of time the whole 'Big Society' affair spanned and how, as a member of the Lords, he could think and plan in decades not years. He had a slightly prophetic sense of himself. I thought back to the 'lords temporal and spiritual' language of his elevation.

I could see this prophetic view both as part of his self-delusion and temporary downfall, and as a splendid robe he drew around himself as protection. He couldn't really admit how much he had been damaged, although the eyes showed it. We parted friends, for which we were both glad.

By 23 September we were close to completing our six-month pilots and held a National Summit of chairpersons and project leaders from all sixteen areas, in the Old Library in Birmingham. It was one of the most exhilarating days of my professional life and I wish I could bottle up all the wisdom of the day and find a way of broadcasting it to every corner of the UK.

We had a series of talks entitled 'My community, what works, what doesn't' by leaders of most of the communities. People were absorbed into the detailed struggle of different parts of the UK and extracted general lessons from many of the brave and inventive solutions.

We had surgeries in which people could learn different skills to transform their communities, from how to write better grant applications, to how to set up a community shop or pub, to how to set up digital communities, time-banking or crowd-sourcing.

An example of the ideas on offer was Jackie Cropper from Grand Central Savings.

Homeless people or people on tough housing estates find it very difficult to get basic banking services and avoid the loan sharks. For example, when poor mothers are given vouchers to get books and clothes for their children for school, they often can't cash them at a bank and so they have to rely on the loan shark, who will give them half its value or less.

Jackie set up banking services on Glasgow estates. Local people, who knew everyone by name, ran these services and they used willing local banks as their back office. This way mothers could get £100 for a £100 voucher. They could also, as Jackie explained, deal with the situation where the guy with the barely disguised weapon in his pocket who shoved them into their estate 'bank' and said, 'She wants to take all her money out' could be given £8 as 'all she has in her account' whereas in reality it was £108.

Paul Twivy, Tessa Jowell and Nick Hurd at the Your Square Mile press launch.

This, for me, graphically describes a reality in Britain that most people never see and a solution that could be replicated across the UK if known about.

We launched the Your Square Mile mutual on 6 October. Nick Hurd and Tessa Jowell both spoke in support of our work. Tessa started life as a community organiser and both feels and understands the vitality of local engagement. Bill Lawns from Pollokshields and Richard Edwards told life as it is on the front-line but also how it could be.

We got very little coverage in the press. I wrote to James

Naughtie and John Humphrys about our launch and they both wrote back to say how much they would like to cover it as a story on the *Today* programme. The editor didn't touch it. If the launch of Britain's first citizens' mutual doesn't warrant any attention from the BBC's flagship news programme then it's difficult to maintain optimism about the media.

Your Square Mile had some notable successes. Across the sixteen areas, we almost doubled regular, constructive contact between citizens and the local authorities; increased, from 50 per cent to 63 per cent, the number of people who felt they could influence local decisions; and increased, from 37 per cent to 50 per cent, the number of people having weekly contact with their neighbours. If this was what we could do in some of the most challenged communities in the UK, imagine what we could do elsewhere.

Yet there is no disguising that we had many failures, including our restrictions as a small team supporting such a wide range of areas. Almost half of all the projects failed immediately because of the lack of confidence of the leaders who had stepped forward in all good faith. They needed the constant support that we were not, sadly, able to provide. What we have learned about the complexity of these areas is hopefully valuable.

£800 million has been poured into Toxteth, for example, since the riots, and four prime ministers have walked through its streets sincerely promising change but not delivering it.

What is good about the area has not, thankfully, been

crushed – the inventiveness, tenacity, diversity and friendliness of its residents. Eighty per cent of Toxteth residents know more than ten neighbours, far more than the average in UK communities. However, the problems with crime, health, housing, addiction and unemployment have barely changed either. Why?

The answers in Toxteth are much the same as they are in all the other areas we approached. Millions have gone into buildings such as community centres but often without consulting the residents about what they wanted. Millions have been poured into charities but often charities that operate in silos for one cause or one ethnic group only.

Some councillors are admired for their tenacity, but the majority of them appear to be invisible in between elections. Many people are simply unaware of local assets. Many community groups and charities are fragile and expend huge amounts of their energy staying alive. Most people don't know the basics of how their area works, how to pull the levers of change.

What do we need to turn these areas around? First of all, we need the rebirth of public meetings and discussions. Not dreary meetings on drizzly Tuesdays at the town hall but the coming together of a wide range of people, especially those six out of ten of us who take no part in civic life, to argue and listen and find new solutions.

Participatory budgeting, when it is handled well, is an excellent example. The evidence in the UK and from around the world is that when people are taken through an iterative, well-facilitated process of prioritising their local budget, they vote for the most vulnerable and needy and drop merely partisan issues.

The UK needs an outpouring of micro-finance to kick-start small local businesses and social enterprises. As Muhammad Yunus, the inventor of micro-credit, said: 'All it needs to get poor people out of poverty is for us to create an enabling environment for them. Once the poor can release their energy and creativity, poverty will disappear very quickly.'

We should be working together to create Community Finance Partnerships that could offer an integrated approach to finance and financial advice for all local/community economic development and social improvement. This Community Finance Partnership could advise on, and use, community shares, credit unions, localgiving.com, the digital charity box Pennies, Givey, crowd-sourcing and time currencies.

We need to be inventive to tackle poverty or scant resources. For example, £3 per resident in an estate of 5,000 people raises £15,000 to kit out a boxing club or a new playground to keep kids fitter, happier and off the street corners.

Time is a currency in the workplace and it should be in volunteering. Spice developed one-hour 'banknotes' that you get for every hour you volunteer. These can then be redeemed against benefits such as free or discounted leisure facilities, sports events, concerts and adult education classes. This is what I held aloft at the Cameron and Clegg meeting in the first week of the coalition.

We need to support the work of food banks such as the excellent Trussell Trust, but also perhaps extend them by finding local people all over the UK who are good cooks, who can prepare cheap but nutritious food and teach others in free, public cookery classes how to do so themselves.

We need neighbours to stop ignoring each other, and in neighbours I include all kinds of institutions and businesses. All over the UK there are millionaires living cheek by jowl with poverty and doing nothing to alleviate it. We have hospices starved for funds in millionaire streets. J. K. Rowling has bravely written *The Casual Vacancy* about these issues.

We need to create a force even greater than the inertia and lack of self-esteem that blights many neighbourhoods. We need a Danny Boyle-style outburst of creative energy. In this regard, we have universities, theatres, art galleries, scientific institutes, orchestras, gyms that too often ignore their physical neighbours.

We need art galleries not to sit behind their Victorian walls but to take copies of their wonderful paintings out on to the streets: galleries can be outdoors and around the streets.

I want to persuade the Hallé Orchestra or the Royal Northern College of Music to work in Moss Side and Hulme, areas they sit in or border, to teach people how to play musical instruments, in the style of Il Sistema and the Simon Bolivar Orchestra in Venezuela.

Can we please have more choirs to bring people together? Can we have more Shakespeare for Schools festivals or Chicken Shed Theatre companies that have put on some of the most moving productions ever, with children who have behavioural problems or physical challenges?

We need businesses to systematically bring their resources to bear in neighbourhoods where they are a significant employer, just as Heineken and Unilever have done with Your Square Mile.

We need to join up the dots of all the various initiatives such as business connectors and community organisers, Community First and Big Local, so that local leaders can understand the 'common ingredients' available to help them to improve their local area.

We need more community markets and 'grow your own' initiatives. We need to really extend the legacy of the Olympics by providing much cheaper or free access to sport for all, as an antidote to the elitism or narrow focus of so many sports clubs.

What I would say to the coalition is that they need to realise that a principle, especially a society-changing principle, isn't a principle until it costs you money.

Eric Pickles and the Department for Communities and Local Government gave £12 million to preserve a bridge, but they couldn't find even £100,000 to support Your Square Mile as one of the most ambitious and active organisations in the country involved in helping communities to strengthen themselves. Nor did they give a single pound to the Manton Community Alliance, who were the very model of what they were trying to achieve.

Britain proved that we are world-class during the Olympics

and Paralympics. We need to apply all that skill, energy and talent to our societal problems and do it with a sense of fun and challenge. Activity and purpose are our redemption.

Chapter 10

Five prime ministers and the politics of their good intentions

P EOPLE ARE COMPLEX AND prime ministers even
more so. It is difficult enough for anyone to pass
through the fame barrier and become 'owned' in some
sense by the public. Friends who have become famous have

commented on the fact that their public persona is not the 'real them' but an outer shell, a projection, a different reality with the same face.

How much more difficult and bizarre it must be to suddenly be the most famous and ever-present person in the country. What is it like to become a surname – Blair, Brown, Cameron – in a thousand headlines? Or even to become an adjective or movement such as 'Thatcherite' or 'Thatcherism'.

Trying to get beyond the headlines to the person themselves and their intent is fascinating and sometimes difficult. I didn't meet Margaret Thatcher, unless you count watching her car being pelted with eggs when she visited our school as Minister of Education, or delivering 250,000 petitions to her famous front door on behalf of the nurses of the UK. Personally, I find the contrived nature of some of her most famous sayings – such as 'You turn if you want to. The lady's not for turning' – self-adoring and stomach-churning.

Often, reading the words without the voice – especially her voice – can allow for a better, more dispassionate understanding. Re-reading her famous speech at the 1980 Brighton conference reveals a lot.

'Our response to disappointment has not been to lengthen our stride but to shorten the distance to be covered.' She (or, more accurately, her speech-writers under her tutelage) knew how to encapsulate and encourage energy and ambition. The language she wanted to use, and did use, was theatrical and vivid.

'Prosperity comes not from grand conferences of economists

but by countless acts of personal self-confidence and self-reliance.' She was powerfully anti-elitist and apparently wanted anyone and everyone to succeed. Yet notice the absence of praise for collaboration and partnership, instead praising the self-reliance of the individual, the grocer, the nation of shopkeepers, from which she came.

'The level of unemployment in our country today is a human tragedy ... Human dignity and self-respect are undermined when men and women are condemned to idleness.' The apparent humanity is lost in the Victorian enmity of the word 'idleness'. The obsession is for the work ethic as the foundation of human dignity whereas many of us would put many other factors higher, such as living true to our values.

Thatcher was, above all, what I would call an 'economeliast'. Just as an existentialist believes that 'existence' precedes 'essence', so Thatcher believed that 'economics' precedes 'essence'...

She said: 'Without a healthy economy we cannot have a healthy society. Without a healthy society the economy will not stay healthy for long.'

The second of these statements is possibly the wisest thing she ever said but sadly she didn't ever put it into practice; she didn't ever put society first. This statement does, however, put paid to the idea that the only thing Thatcher ever thought about society is that 'there is no such thing'.

She may have had iron will and relentless energy in sweeping away the closed shop, restrictive practices, unfettered public spending and inflation. She gave Britain a new energy and purpose. The trouble is that the purpose was one-dimensional and economic.

Fine to let people buy their own council houses as long as you then put as much energy into building new social housing to replace the lost council stock. She didn't; although to be fair, neither did successive governments including New Labour.

If you are going to close down uneconomic coal mines, you cannot close down the people who relied on them for work. You have to imaginatively and supportively rebuild those communities and the self-esteem of the people within them. Yet the ex-mining communities of Glyncoch and Manton with which we worked, and many others throughout the UK, are still carrying the scars from that era.

Thatcher may have been kind to the doormen and cleaners at No. 10. I am sure she lived by a strict moral code. She brilliantly cut through vested interests and red tape and it was great to see her knock aside the tired old patrician Tories. I felt her pain when she left Downing Street for the last time. I hated the cowards who did for her. I was touched by Denis's support. Better the bloodied warrior than the armchair critic. Yet we are still carrying the scars of her lack of care for society as a whole.

John Major once made a significant visit to India and, in a rather brilliant but savage comment, a journalist had described him as 'a splash of grey in a world of colour!'

This was a highly amusing version of a common observation of a Prime Minister who has always seemed dull and safe by comparison with his fiery, iconoclastic predecessor. Yet he was capable of poetry himself and his tale is as curious as the story of Downing Street itself.

The son of a trapeze artist who also ran a garden gnome firm, John Major won a place at Rutlish Grammar School in Merton, south London, but hated it and left school at sixteen with only three O levels.

After being elected to Parliament in 1979, he rose through the ranks, becoming Foreign Secretary, Chancellor of the Exchequer, and eventually Prime Minister in 1990. He was a kind of social mobility incarnate, as indeed was the grocer's daughter who preceded him.

He showed flashes of poetic language during his time in Downing Street, famously describing Britain as a country of 'long shadows on cricket grounds, warm beer, invincible green suburbs, dog lovers and pools fillers and, as George Orwell said, old maids bicycling to Holy Communion through the morning mist'.

Yet John Major has always risked being seen as just a coda to Thatcher's grand symphony. In my very brief personal experience, John Major is not just the quiet, nostalgic cricket-lover and touchstone of an often dry common sense. He has his own brand of humour, irreverence and tenacity. His relationship with Edwina Currie alone refutes the grey stereotype, although clearly not in the manner that either he or Norma would have hoped.

It is difficult to describe anyone as anodyne who can say the following:

Only in Britain could it be thought a defect to be too clever by half. The probability is that too many people are too stupid by three-quarters.

A consensus politician is someone who does something that he doesn't believe is right because it keeps people quiet when he does it.

The sight of allegedly sophisticated politicians parroting complete tripe trivialises and demeans government and it has to be stopped. It's played a significant part in public disillusionment with politics and has led to the absurd situation where more people vote for *Strictly Come Dancing* than voted in the general election.

Society needs to condemn a little more and understand a little less.

'Honest John' bequeathed a much strengthened economy, an economic dividend to New Labour, in the form of low government borrowing (remember that?), falling unemployment and lower interest rates. He laid the foundations for the Good Friday Agreement despite his fierce hatred for Sinn Fein. However, he could never control the rebellions within his own party.

Yet his view of society was wistful, reflective, traditional and, in the end, too passive to make it different, to change its rapidly evolving inequality.

Perhaps he was also too honest and straightforward for the vicious nature of Westminster politics.

There is a remarkable self-awareness and humility about his musing on his own career:

> I shall regret always that I never found my own authentic voice in politics. I was too conservative, too conventional. Too safe, too often. Too defensive. Too reactive.
>
> One abiding regret for me is that ... I did not have the resources to put in place the educational and social changes about which I cared so much; I made only a beginning, and it was not enough.

This was a man who possibly never expected to be Prime Minister and, in his own estimate, let the role govern him, not the other way round.

The opposite was true of his successor, who was often accused of diminishing the role of Parliament by his presidential and 'sofa government' style. Tony Blair was the consummate politician who fell in love with his own prophetic sense of himself. He was almost too naturally gifted as a politician. It was too easy for him to persuade everyone.

He had charm, wit, stamina and a genius for political strategy. He has admitted that his ability to somewhat 'bend' the truth was part of his most patient and substantial achievement: the Good Friday Agreement in 1998.

He admitted in his memoirs to rephrasing one party's view to flatter and fit better with their opponent's. This 'creative ambiguity' as he called it, is possibly a key ingredient in any such process between sworn enemies. Perhaps with tenacity and skill and time, he can still help to achieve peace in the Middle East.

In relation to my anecdote about Downing Street and confusion, if not ineptitude, about when to have tables for meetings and when not, Tony Blair insisted on a diamond-shaped negotiating table for the peace process, allowing for equality, not the adversarial nature of a square or the cosiness of a circle. Who says detail doesn't matter?

How ironic and revealing that when talking of this peace agreement he declared: 'Now is *not* the time for sound bites. I feel the hand of history on my shoulder.' If only he'd had some sort of healthy self-deprecation, some ability to stand back from himself and laugh at this kind of headline-and-history-grabbing obsession.

On the one hand, Blair was a liberator, moderniser and devolver who profoundly affected society. He gave the decision on interest rates to an independent Bank of England; started devolution for Wales and Scotland; he created foundation hospitals and academies that had individual accountability. He was crucial in the development of gay rights and gender and race equality. He banned hunting and he tried to reform the House of Lords and the Lord Chancellorship.

Yet he presided over excessively tight message control within his party, and set up obsessive metrics for public services, with all the attendant bureaucracy. He also had very few modernisers within his team, inheriting many of them from the Kinnock era.

His introduction of the minimum wage, windfall tax on privatised utilities, the New Deal for the unemployed and tax credits spoke of zeal to help the poor.

Yet many of these were the legacy of John Smith and/or the obsession of his redistributive Chancellor, and social mobility didn't noticeably improve in his decade in office. He didn't really start to deliver his personal 'choice and diversity' agenda until his second or third term.

Of course, foreign policy ultimately defined Blair, and Kosovo and Sierra Leone were successful and skilful interventions. The post-9/11 invasions of Afghanistan and Iraq were something else.

We all experienced 9/11 as something close to apocalyptic, unfolding before our eyes. It seemed that stabbing at America's heart, with such synchronised and targeted cruelty, might feasibly unleash the end of the world as a reaction. That may still prove to be true: the lighting of a long and deadly fuse.

America has led the free world for a long time and is an elder brother to the UK. To see this parent of freedom so vulnerable was as shocking in its way as seeing your own parents as fragile. In the aftermath of these extraordinary events, Blair became both stronger and weaker as he moved on to the global stage.

Alastair Campbell famously said of the Blair government, 'We don't do God.'

How much healthier it would have been if Campbell, and others lassoing and binding the party to its strict message-control post, had let Tony Blair 'do God' in public. Then we might have heard more of his true thoughts, seen clearly the religious pact one suspects he had with George W. Bush on Iraq, the prophetic sense of fighting evil and of being a saviour. Then we might have asked more penetrating questions of the WMD claims laid in front of us.

What always worried me about Tony Blair was his desire to always be presidentially central; to rely on the brilliance of sound bites and statistics; to mine anything within himself, including very personal matters, in order to deliver a powerful speech.

He is undoubtedly, though, one of the most gifted politicians Britain has ever known. Some of his greatest and bravest achievements were purely political but important. He was brave enough to take on the unions, to tackle Clause Four, which wedded the party to nationalisation, and to reinvent his party in a manner that won three elections in a row.

He did achieve great things in Northern Ireland, building though he did on John Major's achievements. He had foreign policy successes such as Kosovo. He attacked the poor standards of state education with academies. He introduced the minimum wage. He did invest in new hospitals, schools and social housing, replacing many decaying buildings and revitalising the landscape.

He presided over a period of economic growth. He also increased welfare spending and reduced poverty, although, significantly, not inequality. With Iraq, however, he saw black-and-white morality where others saw a horrible blood and oil-soaked technicolor.

People are revealed by their actions and Tony Blair has spent recent years amassing an estimated £75 million fortune by delivering speeches and advice around the world through his company Tony Blair Associates, sometimes with very suspect regimes. This is all the more surprising for Cherie's protestation, when he resigned, that he was likely to devote himself to pro bono causes.

He has, to be fair, channelled some of his fortune into the Tony Blair Foundation, which sponsors international programmes to combat religious extremism. This is revealing of his true centre of gravity: his faith. We should also acknowledge his work in trying to improve governance in Africa and to promote Palestinian economic growth. These are vital and thoughtful causes.

A demonised Blair is a haunted Blair and therefore a less potent Blair. We need a potent Blair to do good in the world, especially if he can apply the skills he applied relentlessly and patiently to Northern Ireland to the Middle East. Then history will judge him well, if fatally flawed in his decisions on Iraq.

As must be apparent from my earlier chapters, I think that Gordon Brown has been seriously misjudged. From my own contact with him and numerous acts he has undertaken, many of them quietly, I judge him to be a man driven by a passion for equality and social justice not only in the UK but also around the world.

That he was paradoxical there can be no doubt. Will Hutton memorably described him as 'a friend of the poor who did much for the rich and a democrat who feared elections'.

He divided responsibility for the banking and monetary system between the Bank of England and the Financial Services Authority and famously believed in only light-touch regulation of the markets: a conversion to 'neoconservative economics.' These were crucial mistakes in creating the credit boom and subsequent crash.

What made this worse was his Canute-like statement as Chancellor that there would be no more boom and bust. He also sold off 60 per cent of Britain's gold reserves at rock bottom prices and diminished pensions by taxing the dividends on their investments.

Pitted against this, he was a prime architect in decisively saving the global banking system. He did much to tackle third-world debt. He was quick to understand globalisation and the new economic world order. People have talked about squandering the proceeds of the golden tax harvests, but actually Brown did invest in education, health and science and we have this legacy on our daily landscape: new and better schools and hospitals.

Although the tax take under Blair and Brown went up from 39.3 per cent of GDP to 42.4 per cent in 2006, often by complex, indirect and stealthy means, it was spent in a genuinely redistributive way via tax credits, child benefit, income support and financial support to pensioners.

Although most chancellors are centralists by nature, Gordon Brown proposed moving powers from the Prime Minister to Parliament, such as the power to declare war, so crucial post-Iraq. He also proposed a rebalance of power between

Westminster and local government and moving power from Parliament to citizens.

Gordon Brown's idea for citizen juries, although mocked by the opposition as focus groups under another name, was a powerful idea worth now revisiting. A citizens' jury would a group of between twelve and twenty people, chosen to represent the communities from which they come. They would be asked to look at real issues, in the same way as a jury does in a courtroom.

The juries would spend a day, or several days, considering the chosen subject. They would be given facts and figures that have been independently verified and would hear evidence from a range of experts. Jurors would then discuss the issues among themselves before reaching a conclusion. Their decisions would be used to help advise ministers on policy.

The level of informed debate in the Scottish referendum and the success of participatory budgeting done properly – opening up facts about local spending issues and encouraging citizens to co-prioritise and allocate them – prove the power of getting citizens involved in tough policy issues.

It is always said of Gordon Brown that he flunked the opportunity to hold a snap election in November 2007. However, if you have waited as long as he did to take over the top post, you would have to think very carefully about potentially losing it after five months.

It may be true to say that he was temperamentally unsuited to being PM in some ways. However, imagine the intense pressure of the post, combined with the desire to master detail, combined with being blind in one eye and with continual and excessive tiredness. Add in the stress of your first child dying, your son being diagnosed with cystic fibrosis and the Prince Charles-style wait to get the top job, and I think temper is an understandable if regrettable by-product.

Not only has Gordon Brown remained a dedicated local MP for Kirkcaldy and Cowdenbeath, a post he will sadly leave in 2015, he has also held unpaid positions on the World Wide Web Foundation to involve disadvantaged communities, at the World Economic Forum and as a United Nations Special Envoy on Global Education.

Perhaps his most revealing recent role was in the Scottish referendum. His voice when Chancellor and PM was often muffled, his speaking style could be too akin to baroque architecture: too complex. Yet on subjects about which he is passionate – tackling inequality and the future of Scotland within the British family being two such examples – he is eloquent, sharp and incisive. He is the most value-driven Prime Minister we have had in the post-war era and certainly the most misunderstood.

I have already said much about David Cameron in my 'Big Society' chapters. I have had an odd and sometimes difficult relationship with him. I was asked with Nat Wei to lead many aspects of his flagship ideology of the Big Society. It quickly became clear to me that the only way the Big Society would succeed was by a constructive citizen rebellion: to challenge politicians to a new kind of relationship with those they supposedly represent.

It was clearly not going to succeed as the ideology of a Tory Prime Minister in the middle of a recession anywhere outside of the Home Counties.

This is why I was so adamant about the Big Society Network being independent. That's why I left it as soon as it became apparent that it wasn't going to be allowed to be independent. I was lambasted in *The Guardian* when I said that despite all the Big Society failings, I felt Cameron was sincere in his intentions. I still hold to this view. I don't believe that it was just a fig leaf for the shrinking state. He persisted in defending it for far too long after it became toxic for it to be a purely cynical idea. However, sincerity itself can be deceptive. It can lead you down the wrong path. If cherished too much it can stop you listening to the sincere criticism of others.

There is something deep in Cameron's upbringing that commits him to traditional morality and public service. He is a quiet Christian. His father, Ian, was born with both legs deformed and clearly dealt with this blow with great courage and dignity, which must have been very inspiring. David Cameron is obviously a devoted father and the nights he spent sleeping on the floor of a hospital ward next to his disabled son Ivan speak volumes about why he is committed to the NHS, even if he went the wrong way about protecting it, via a disastrous, top-down reorganisation.

One of the main problems is that Cameron's social experience is too narrow, and in saying that, I am not trying to reduce him to a social stereotype. I was struck in the meeting at Somerset House in which he defended the Big Society for the nth time at how his frame of reference was the volunteers of polite Oxfordshire villages. He couldn't possibly know (as, frankly, neither could I before I got involved) the chronic and overlapping problems of, for example, Glyncoch, Moss Side and Toxteth.

He has been described by comedy writer Charlie Brooker as 'a hollow Easter egg with no bag of sweets inside'. This is to do him an injustice but there is something unclear now about his own core purpose. He got a First Class degree from Oxford and yet never appears to be an intellectual heavyweight. Like Blair, he often seems to use his intelligence to be politically pragmatic and skilful.

What is particularly sad is that the Cameron who took over the Tory Party leadership in 2005 with a reforming zeal seems to have disappeared or gone on a long retreat. Where is the man who wanted to reinvent the right; fight for more women in politics; put the environment at the top of all agendas; forge a new deal between citizens and government; radically devolve power? Was it always just a ploy to get into power? Was it an imitation of Blair but only of his political skill? If Blair was, in some ways, 'Thatcher Lite' is Cameron actually 'Thatcher Max?'

It has been a huge privilege to work with the last three prime ministers on vital social change. Now I want to paint a picture of how I think Downing Street and Parliament can and must change in relation to its citizens and how we must all change in our relationship to power if we are to create a genuine democracy and tackle the huge issues that face us as a society.

PART TWO

A NEW KIND OF POLITICS AND A STRONGER SOCIETY

Chapter 11

A federal and digital Britain

THE SCOTTISH REFERENDUM HAS catalysed a UK-wide series of issues and changes that are not simply constitutional in nature. They also work on a number of layers. Firstly, there is the difficult issue of balancing devolved Scottish, Welsh, Northern Irish and now, it seems, possibly English parliaments with having UK-wide decision-making power on cross-border issues and a combined clout in the world.

Parliament's resolution of the West Lothian question is especially tricky. There is talk of an English Parliament in Birmingham. Can this really make sense, however, if there is to continue to be a UK Parliament? England makes up 84 per cent of the population of the United Kingdom. Having both could be costly and inefficient.

It seems much more sensible to have a UK Parliament at Westminster with English-only sessions and voting on specifically English issues. The West Lothian question is being overstated because it suits the Tories to do so. Since 1919, there have been only three elections when the ruling party of the UK government has not also won a majority in purely English constituencies. Of 5,000 Commons votes since 1997, only twenty-one depended on Scottish MPs.

As the Speaker has pointed out, once devo-max becomes effective in Scotland, a new convention would operate in Westminster in which Scottish MPs would not vote on the devolved issues.

A genuinely federalist United Kingdom is possible and could be desirable, balancing localism and centrality, bringing decision-making closer to home and recognising the vitally different circumstances of the four nations and even of different English regions. Trying to make it happen is not easy but the current system is a recipe for confusion.

In Scotland, there are 129 MSPs: Members of the Scottish Parliament. They represent seventy-three constituencies with one MSP apiece and another eight regions with seven MSPs apiece. Then there are fifty-nine Scottish Members of the UK

Parliament with different constituencies. There was a recommendation by the Arbuthnott Commission in 2006 to review all boundaries together. Of course, like so many common-sense suggestions in the world of politics, it has been ignored. MSPs can also be Scottish Members of the UK Parliament but most aren't. Confused? You should be.

It is incredibly difficult to get people involved in politics at the best of times. If you are a Scottish voter, you have to contact your MSP on devolved matters and your MP on non-devolved matters. Their geographical constituencies may overlap but will be different one from the other, as well as being responsible for different policies.

Surely this needs to be easier: for example, just one MP for each agreed constituency in the United Kingdom, who both sits in the Scottish, Welsh, English (or regional English) and Northern Irish parliaments to decide on devolved matters and in the UK Parliament to decide on UK-wide matters. It's easier for constituents to have one MP and it enables that MP to have a holistic understanding of both the UK and the local issues. It saves money and duplication.

A number of people have argued for some time, notably the Liberal Democrats, that England needs regional assemblies or parliaments, with manageable population sizes not dissimilar to those of Scotland.

Yorkshire, for example, is England's biggest county, has the same population as Scotland and an economy twice the size of Wales but it has the powers of neither, according to the Yorkshire First campaign.

You can also make a case for much smaller self-governing regions that have a distinctive culture, history and geography, such as Cornwall and the Scottish islands.

My personal view is that a good starting point would be to have a north of England and a Midlands assembly because there are strong, identifiable needs.

Northern England and many areas of the Midlands have suffered massively from the decline in manufacturing and mining and need special attention to create new, thriving economies.

They would also be able to focus on the regional infrastructure needed as a bedrock, be that a high-speed, cross-Pennine train service – the so-called HS3 – or fibre optic broadband in rural areas. The 'One North' plan launched by Leeds, Manchester, Liverpool, Sheffield and Newcastle embodies this line of thinking.

In addition to this regional focus, we need to release the power of individual cities such as Glasgow, Manchester, Birmingham, Liverpool, Newcastle, Leeds, Bristol, Cardiff and Belfast to engage their citizens and self-determine much more of their own future.

It is baffling and damning to see how limply the coalition presented the case for more directly elected mayors in England and Wales, despite it potentially being one of the most tangible manifestations of the Tories' 'Big Society' ideas and of the cherished 'localism' of the Liberal Democrats.

The idea of more elected mayors has been proposed by a number of politicians in the past, including Michael Heseltine and John Major. The Blair government's commitment to reform local government in London led to the establishment of the first elected Mayor of London in 2000. Thirteen directly elected mayoralties in other cities were then created between 2002 and 2010.

Using the powers in the much-trumpeted Localism Act 2011, on 3 May 2012, referendums were held in ten English cities to decide whether or not to switch to a system that includes a directly elected mayor. Of the ten given the chance, only Bristol voted for a new mayoral system. Doncaster also held a vote and confirmed their existing arrangement of having an elected mayor.

I suspect the apathy and rejection was a combination of a poor to non-existent explanation by the government worn out by the rejection of the Big Society, a knuckling down by most people simply trying to survive the recession, and a widespread belief that nothing could really change an out-of-touch and morally dubious political system.

This is an especially sad result when you consider how much elected mayors have achieved around the world.

Many of us are aware of the huge impact made by successive Mayors of New York. Famously, Rudy Giuliani and, less famously, his predecessor, David Dinkins, dramatically cut crime in New York by applying a 'zero-tolerance' approach to minor misdemeanours such as graffiti, turnstile jumping and 'squeegee men' intimidating motorists into paying them for cleaning windscreens.

The so-called Broken Windows theory on which it was based is that a well-ordered environment discourages further vandalism and decay and that petty crime inexorably leads to more significant crime. The effects were notable, if also controversial, and, according to some, difficult to disentangle from other beneficial factors such as rising employment.

In London, Ken Livingstone and Boris Johnson have both had a significant impact in and beyond London. Yet there are also many lesser-known but equally charismatic mayors across the world who have imaginatively transformed their cities in recent years, proving how potent a post it can be.

San Antonio's mayor ran huge, live events for thousands of citizens at a time, to decide the city's budget.

Bogota's former mayor, Antanas Mockus, asked its citizens to voluntarily pay 10 per cent extra tax, and 63,000 did. He halved traffic deaths by painting the street where people died and employing 400 mime artists to illustrate the dangers of jaywalking.

Oklahoma's mayor transformed his city's waistline by personally fronting a campaign to 'lose 1 million lb'.

Helsinki has delivered the guarantee of a job, study or training place for every young person, and participatory budgeting was started in a single city in Brazil – Porto Alegre – determined to make its meagre city budgets the most effective they could be in tackling its huge social problems, by involving the people themselves in voting on priorities.

Not only do we need to resurrect and properly present the idea of more elected mayors, we also need to move beyond the stereotypical local authority candidate and encourage a much broader cross-section of people to stand for election.

London is a global city, almost a state in its own right, more different to the rest of the UK than even New York is to the average Midwest town. The inequality between London and the rest of the UK in terms of property prices, demographics and indeed culture is unhealthy for the UK and for London itself. London is being strangled by its own rising prices and becoming dangerously dependent on foreign investment and the discredited banking sector.

A generation is now growing up that will not ever be able to afford to buy property in London. If the mansion tax comes into being, many asset-rich but modest-income families will be forced into selling their homes. The benefits freeze the Tories have suggested for two years from April 2016 will cost a family with children and one or more parents in work close to £500 a year, which makes a massive difference to those already stretched. What is the combined effect of all this misery? A massive exodus from London and a hollowed-out city full of the rich and foreign, often absent, owners.

It is clear that the council tax bands need to be re-evaluated, however arduous the task. Council tax should rise steeply for houses in excess of £2 million. They will still be way below the mansion tax. We should plough much of the extra money raised into building affordable housing. We need to charge both an investment tax and capital gains on foreign, absentee owners and stop our city being raped for property assets.

In addition we need to build up industry, employment, infrastructure and housing, but also the arts, sport, leisure and entertainment in the north, the Midlands and the south-west of England. We need other world-class cities in England, in the fully rounded sense of that term. This would have the minor benefit of bringing in more tourist income and the major benefit of building the civic pride and happiness of those cities and drawing more people away from London, thus bringing down house prices.

Highlighting the need for change, the UK has one of the most centralised systems of public finance of any OECD country. I have already talked about how big, impersonal and unwieldy our local government is. An average local authority in England and Wales covers 147,000 people: 50 per cent more than the average American county. What's worse is their lack of spending autonomy.

The amount of tax set by local government accounts for just 1.7 per cent of Britain's GDP, compared to 5 per cent in France and 16 per cent in Sweden. Local authorities receive the majority of their funding from central government, with only one-quarter coming from their local council tax. This makes them especially vulnerable to Westminster and they have had the largest cuts during the recession: 28 per cent since 2010 plus an additional and crushing 2.9 per cent in 2014/15. Power and budgets need to be devolved, to enable people to feel empowered.

Our concentric circles of identity can, for example, be described as:

- Individual lives in households.

- Community members of a street or neighbourhood.

- Residents of a village, town or city.

- People who live in a distinctive region of a country.

- Citizens of a country.

- Citizens of the world.

Each level of identity and influence affects the next 'ring' in a constant rolling out and rolling in from the micro to the macro and back again.

For example, telling people that a fifth of the stock market is owned by their investments in unit trusts, insurance companies and pension funds gives them some sense of how they might use the power of their individual savings to promote ethical investments and business practices such as fair trade.

Breaking down their individual household tax bill into its component parts – e.g. 'This year you paid £1,600 for defence; £2,800 for the health service' – might run the risk of their resentment of certain items but, more importantly, it makes them think about their priorities and values, about their individual relationship to government. It removes the passive anonymity of giving dollops of money through the PAYE system. We will see how much the coalition government have adopted my ideas on this, if at all.

If we had more directly elected mayors to represent and

change cities; a north of England, Midlands, Northern Irish and Welsh Assembly as well as the Scottish and UK parliaments, we would move forward on a much more democratic basis.

A key principle in all of this is to create wards, local authorities and, ultimately, constituencies that citizens themselves feel make sense.

In all the nineteen communities where Your Square Mile has worked, we have taken large-scale maps into our public meetings and agreed the exact physical boundaries of our pilot areas. There has rarely been any dissent amongst the fifty to seventy people in each area. People easily agree which parks, schools, shopping areas etc. fall within their area. Many in local authorities would like to see boundaries redrawn on this citizen-friendly basis.

In addition to the structured layers of influence, from neighbourhoods up to countries, we need to harness the power of broadcasting and digital technology to demonstrate to people the aggregated power of simple, individual human actions to shape our world, and indeed save it.

Google Earth is a paradigm of this way of thinking: we can move from the globe down to an individual house and back out again in a matter of seconds.

Digital technology, ranging from mobiles to iPods to the internet, has so often trapped us in bubbles of isolation, virtual contact not real contact. It has threatened to separate the generations into 'digiphiles' or 'digital natives' and 'digital sceptics' and 'digital illiterates'.

We need to promote the use of digital technology to connect. This could take many forms. We could, for example, encourage flash mobbing on mobiles as a means of instantly organising people to help with a disaster such as a flood.

We could use social media or wireless networks as a means of connecting everyone in every street for social purposes – be it through Google or Facebook groups, by community or micro-broadcasting – so that no elderly or disabled or simply lonely person in a street is isolated. This local use of social media is now happening in many Big Lunch streets and neighbourhoods.

We can stage government-led national, regional or local debates on key issues with the aid of broadcasters and the internet, in which people can interactively express opinions and vote; delivering a powerful sense of being consulted, of instant democracy, of government taking on board the opinions of citizens. The biggest single example of this is the National Health Service.

Health service managers predict that the NHS will go into deficit this year or next and the NHS Confederation has said that an extra £2 billion a year is needed in England alone to simply maintain current levels of service. Monitor, the health regulator, has estimated a £5 billion funding gap in 2015/16 for NHS England. In addition, the NHS in Wales is facing an estimated £2.5 billion funding gap over the next decade and in Scotland there is a funding gap of £400 million to £450 million in the next two financial years, 2015–17. So-called trolley waits to get into A&E have tripled since 2011.

Solutions such as charging to see a GP or paying up to £75 a night for a stay in hospital are being mooted. There are other ways. It is estimated that at least £5 billion a year is wasted on NHS inefficiencies. A hospital in Seattle shows how much of this waste can be eliminated: involve all your staff in honestly admitting mistakes and solving problems collectively by observation.

The Virginia Mason Hospital in Seattle encourages all 5,600 of its staff to report problems without any fear of repercussions. In 2002, its CEO, Dr Gary Kaplan, was inspired by a visit to Toyota in Tokyo, where anyone with a problem can pull a cord and stop the whole production line whilst everyone gathers round to solve the problem with them.

After the death of a patient in 2004 due to a mistake in administering drugs during a critical operation, the hospital adopted a similar process called Patient Safety Alerts. They also look for continuous improvements. By putting supplies where staff needed them, they reduced the average number of steps taken by a nurse every day from 10,000 to 1,200. This has allowed nurses to spend 90 per cent of their time with patients, compared to the US hospital average of 35 per cent.

Electronic sensors were put in beds to alert nurses when a patient started to sit up in bed, to intervene before any risk of a fall. Separate corridors have been introduced for staff and patients rather than both muddling along the same space, speeding up movement.

This is all built on observation and a culture of problem-solving. We could encourage this not just within individual hospital sites in the UK but between them as well. Porters, cleaners, nurses and many others can help to make the NHS safer and more efficient, and gain job satisfaction and pride from doing so.

Similarly, why can't the public be involved in debating and voting on ways in which more money could be saved in, or contributed to, the NHS. Perhaps better-off people would be happy to pay for prescriptions, for example, instead of being exempt. Perhaps we could develop local health ISAs so that those people with savings – often those over the age of fifty – can contribute part of those savings into a fund that invests in their local hospital.

Much of this collaborative approach could take place online, where the problems and possible solutions could be well visualised, explained and discussed. It would become all the more powerful, however, if such discussion also took place in local public meetings.

The same principles apply to other areas of need. For example, if you want to improve traffic flow in a city, the best way to do it is to have a live network of observations and ideas by taxi and bus drivers, traffic wardens and lollipop ladies. If you want to tackle crime, have a similar live network for posties and other delivery service people. We are all potential problem-solvers.

If you want a productive society, don't bombard people with GDP per head statistics: give them something they believe in. As we struggle to reconcile ourselves in the UK to a smaller economic role in the world, as our cultural identities become more varied and complex, why don't we set ourselves the goal of being world leaders in other ways? Why don't we try to become world leaders in genuine, digital-enabled democracy or in equality of opportunity and social mobility?

Scotland has shown that it has a commitment to a fair and just society with excellent education and health available to all. It seems to have a stronger sense of self and a stronger vision of society than the English.

Politics itself needs to change, but it also needs new attitudes to, and alliances with, both civic society and business.

Chapter 12

The core purpose of business

BUSINESSES HAVE ALWAYS BEEN the victims of revolutionaries seeking to change society: from Lenin almost 100 years ago to Greenpeace today, business often comes under attack.

Supposing businesses, some of which are more powerful than national governments, and many of which are global in reach, were to become the revolutionaries instead, harnessing their size and power for good?

Supposing businesses led new solutions to societal problems? Supposing companies ran into the arms of what is most needed and most challenging and thereby built stronger revenues? For this to happen we need a fundamental rethink.

'CSR' stands for 'corporate social responsibility' and it is now numbingly predictable and should be declared dead, or at least restricted and outmoded, as a mode of thinking and operating. Business needs to get behind something more fundamental that will contribute significantly to society, and which is more creative, more allied to its commercial objectives and more engaging. I would argue this should be called core purpose. Business is, after all, named after the word 'busyness', the process of being busy. To what purpose are we busy?

As a concept, corporate social responsibility deadens the soul. 'Corporate' suggests something slow and cumbersome that only takes place in headquarters buildings, rather than out in the real world. 'Responsibility' is a 'must do' rather than a 'want to do' word.

Whilst it was a vital development in business thinking at the time, most CSR now follows a very predictable and limited pattern. Most companies who pursue it have a nominated annual charity, encourage payroll giving and give their employees one or two paid days a year in which to volunteer. The choice of charities is often generic and populist: big, well-marketed cancer and children's charities are usually chosen rather than the smaller, more local charities that are in greater need of both time and money.

Volunteering is often justified on the basis of 'team-building', ignoring the equally important fact that it is 'individual-building'. Corporate volunteering is usually restricted to simple, physical tasks such as repainting hospices, community centres or playgrounds or clearing and planting areas of land. These are the easiest activities to organise and they also have the benefit of providing a tangible, gratifying result. For many people, these activities also get them away from a sedentary job in front of a computer.

This is good, important volunteering, don't get me wrong, but it is the stuff of worthy paragraphs and standard, smiley photos in annual reports and sadly it is often peripheral tokenism and can even be a partial eclipse of a company's real energy.

I am not suggesting that it should be abandoned but rather that it should be incorporated into something much more vibrant and holistic that is truly transformational.

Companies are falling over themselves to prove to their consuming public how ethically sound they are. Don't, however, confuse activity, or worse, fluff, with progress. Existentialists believe that existence precedes essence. It is important for businesses to believe that action – doing good things – must precede advertising and ethical marketing. To corrupt Gandhi, 'Business must be the change it claims to be making in the world.'

The financial services sector, trying to cleanse itself of the 'bankster' associations of the global economic meltdown, is at the front of the queue in claiming newly enlightened, ethical behaviour.

In some instances, this is being pursued vigorously, in the face of many obstacles, not least sceptical employees as well as cynical consumers. A case in point is Antony Jenkins, the CEO of Barclays, who is relentlessly driving through a programme of reform to detoxify the bank, despite the public derision of his own investment banking team and the tsunami of mis-selling scandals hitting his industry. I admire what Mr Jenkins is doing because he is doing it thoroughly and transparently and in the knowledge it will take years.

The Co-op Bank is trying to recover, variously, from the cocaine-, ketamine- and gay-orgy-loving Methodist minister turned councillor turned banker who was their chairman; foolishly merging with the debt-ridden Britannia building society; and the subsequent £1.5 billion black hole in its finances. It is now 70 per cent owned by two American hedge funds.

One of its first decisions under new ownership was to run a TV ad in which a clean-living alpha male (i.e. not Paul Flowers) – who apparently is a Co-op Bank employee – mysteriously strips off and has the word 'Ethics' tattooed onto his body. The ad looks like a mixture between a Bond movie trailer and a Gillette shaving ad, but comes with the claim that for over twenty years the Co-op Bank has refused to lend £1 billion to would-be clients who didn't match their ethical criteria.

The track record in ethical investment is impressive even if the ad does its best to confuse. It will be interesting to see if the hedge-fund owners will stick by the ethical history of the bank even when it means sacrificing revenue and profit. Strangely, if they do persist with ethics, they will put many banks to shame and deservedly, and ironically, unearth a goldmine.

I was at a stakeholder event held by a major bank last year. In the Q&A, someone persistently asked the question 'Can you please tell me the role of a modern bank in a simple sentence?' The panel of senior bank managers struggled to answer, as do many of their competitors. Since many of our current woes come from the banking crisis, it's useful to look back to the fundamentals of banking to answer that question.

Banks started with loans of grain to farmers and traders. Repayment was made from the subsequent harvest. Banking then grew with, and supported, trade: from trading obsidian for Stone Age tools to copper and silver. In Greece and then the Roman Empire, temples were the places where treasure was deposited and responsible money-lending took place: they were the most trustworthy places and the centre of financial as well as religious life, an interesting combination and one worth noting in the modern, often amoral, financial world.

Later, banking grew up around the '*agora*': the Roman markets in which moneylenders set up stalls in enclosed court-yards. These were on long benches called *bancu,* or later *banca* in Italian, from which the English 'bank' and Spanish *banco* are derived. Bankrupt and being 'broke' derive from the Italian *banca rotta* meaning 'broken bench', which is what happened when a merchant banker lost his traders' deposits.

Lending and banking was tangible, local, based on trust. Then things started to change, become more sophisticated but less tangible. Bills of exchange emerged to avoid the cost and complication of transporting gold under guard. Goldsmiths in London discovered they could lend more than the gold and silver coin they had on hand by lending paper receipts: the birth of so-called fractional reserve banking.

From this point onwards, banking became less about coins and goods and more about clever mechanisms that have ended in the modern day in complex instruments such as derivatives and futures, where the connections between the money invested, the investment and its return have become increasingly confused. The relationships have also gone from local and face-to-face to global and digital. This has often resulted in a clever and often disastrous form of gambling.

This brief history helps to define the core purpose of banks, something they have often failed to clarify for themselves. As Bruce Judson, senior fellow at Yale, said:

> Banks in a capitalist society are meant to create wealth and decrease risk. Finance is an intermediary good. You cannot eat it, experience it or physically use it. The purpose is to support other activities in the economy, to allocate money to the people or entities that will create the greatest wealth for the overall society.

If you accept that capitalism can be moral, then the purpose of banks is societal.

James Dempsey at the Centre for the Study of Global Ethics has put the case even more clearly:

> It is a mistake to think of banks only as associations of private individuals engaged in market activity. Banks are institutions with multiple stakeholder groups that are embedded in the institutional framework of society and that benefit from this position. society depends on the ongoing ability of banks to provide these functions.

In other words, there is a symbiosis between society and banks. Banks have a societal 'licence to operate'.

This, in my mind, is the key role of modern banks: to spot and support human potential and need in a non-political and fair manner. The reason that we have banks rather than governments lending all the money is that the government would tend to lend to the important and well connected and ignore the needs of the ordinary citizen or the poor. Banks, please note!

The think tank Respublica has recently suggested that there should be a Bankers' Oath similar to the doctors' Hippocratic Oath. It would commit bankers to 'exhibit a duty of care above and beyond what is required by law' and to 'engender the responsible creation of value'.

Respublica even talks about 'the joy that comes from supporting the needs of society', which I believe is both truthful and powerful, even if it is so far removed from the current world of £20 billion of PPI mis-selling and the rigging of Libor, foreign exchange and gold markets. An oath is, in one sense, just a more committed version of an ethical mission statement. Yet Holland has enshrined such a Bankers' Oath in law. Perhaps we should follow suit.

A wider and wider group of people in government, encouraged by think tanks and international best practice, are also realising that we need a much more diversified financial sector. We have a very narrow range of financial services dominated by plcs. We need more mutuals and we need to strengthen existing mutuals.

There is a lot of evidence to show that a mixed financial system is much more stable. Diversity would reduce the pricing power of conventional banks and raise standards. Five EU countries, including France, have 40 per cent or more of their banking sector run by co-operatives and mutuals. In the UK, building societies account for just 3 per cent of banking assets. UK mutuals used to provide 90 per cent of our insurance market. Now it's 7.5 per cent. The global average is 25 per cent. We invented modern mutuality but have now largely abandoned it.

We have stereotyped mutuals as friendly but unsophisticated. Mutuality is associated with building societies from gritty, northern towns: trustworthy but assumed to be narrow in their range of services and skills. Nothing could be further from the truth. 2.5p extra in every £1 of insurance premium goes to the customers themselves if they use a mutual. It costs, on average, 35 per cent more to run a plc than a mutual.

Mutual providers deliver a 2–8 per cent higher return on annuities. Some of the most sophisticated and demanding consumers in the world choose to use mutual providers, including the French, Japanese, Scandinavians and Americans.

All de-mutualised financial providers have lost efficiency and reduced their service standards post conversion to a plc. Time and time again we have allowed excellent, mutual financial providers to be turned into plcs for a quick windfall. A major bank could be turned into a mutual. TSB, with its trustee savings bank heritage, would be a logical choice. After all, they were started by a vicar in Dumfries to help the working poor of his parish.

In order to grow, building societies and other mutuals need to be allowed to raise capital in different ways, such as redeemable shares. Rather than just lend to individuals, building societies could be encouraged to lend to businesses, especially SMEs. They could also be allowed by the Financial Conduct Authority to lend more to those people who are on lower incomes.

This look back at banking history and the importance of mutual institutions is a useful context for other business sectors. If businesses are to transform their relationship to their employees and to society at large, they need to look back to the companies that spearheaded the Industrial Revolution and created consumerism. It is notable that these Victorian businesses saw their role as being societies in and of themselves as well as contributing to society at large.

Jeremiah James Colman, who founded Colman's of Norwich 200 years ago, created an entire society within his company. The company provided a school for the children of the workers, a clothing club, religious services, evening classes, a reading society, outings and a work band. They were the first company in the world to employ an industrial nurse. Jeremiah's wife supervised cheap and nutritious meals in the canteen. They also set up a trust fund from which impoverished employees could claim in times of hardship.

Of course, there was no welfare state and therefore companies had to provide many of these services if they were to keep their workers healthy and motivated. Nonetheless, Jeremiah Colman's funeral brought Norwich to a standstill, with shops closed out of respect and half the 3,000-strong workforce following the hearse on foot. How many modern CEOs would have employees at their funerals? Very few, one suspects, but perhaps such a desire should guide them.

Colman's is now part of the mighty Unilever empire, and William Hesketh Lever, one of Unilever's eponymous founders, also created an entire society in his own company. In 1887, he decided that his soap business had outgrown its original factory in Warrington. In planning where to expand, Lever always had it in mind to build his workers a village rather than simply building a factory. When he founded the village of Port Sunlight, named after his soap brand, he was aware that the standard of housing in Birkenhead and Liverpool was deplorable and that well-housed workers would be happy and productive employees.

Lever's aim 'was not directly financial but to establish friendly relations between capital and labour, to get them to do their best work, to make men's comfort depend on the firm's prosperity and to put capital in the right by treating men as well as possible, leaving it to their conscience to repay'.

This is the language of mutual self-interest. There's nothing sentimental about it. Indeed, the story is that if a worker took a day off work because of sickness, he or she had to display their workers' boots on the porch. Because they only possessed one pair of boots – provided by the company – Lever could patrol the houses in Port Sunlight, look for the boots and know that the workers concerned were genuinely ill and not down at the pub! Good businesses run like good families – trusting and knowing in equal measure – not at the extremes of the wholly pure or the wholly commercial.

Lever introduced profit sharing for his workers: an early John Lewis. He believed that long hours of work were inhuman and unproductive, and pioneered the eight-hour working day. Membership of the holiday club was compulsory! There were twenty-eight different clubs and societies in Port Sunlight and Lever's work outings became the biggest picnics in the world. He took all 2,000 workers to London for Queen Victoria's Diamond Jubilee in 1897.

The examples of Colman's of Norwich and Unilever in Port Sunlight highlight the vital role that businesses can play as local citizens.

Set up thirty years ago, Business in the Community is 'working to shape a new contract between business and society, in order to secure a fairer society and a more sustainable future'. They employ more than 400 people and work with over 330 senior business leaders.

Yet, when Your Square Mile surveyed the British public in 2013, 60 per cent of people think businesses should definitely increase their involvement with community life. Only one in twelve people rate business's current contribution to their community as being very good or excellent. Four out of ten think it's either poor or very poor.

The benefits of business getting more involved in community support are not just warm and fuzzy. Fifty-four per cent of people said they would be more likely to buy the product/use the services of a company that is genuinely involved with their village, town or city. The now troubled Tesco discovered that when they delivered much clearer, more in-depth and practical support to the communities around their worst-performing stores, the commercial performance of those stores noticeably improved.

What communities want from businesses is much more imaginative, and sometimes simpler, than the usual assumption of money and volunteers. It includes use of land and buildings; help with grant applications and accounts; free legal advice; spare or discarded IT equipment.

Health and safety rules have turned many factories that previously had community interaction and schools visits into isolated fortresses. Whilst we need to keep people safe, there is a far greater need for businesses to be visited by the community and vice versa.

Paul Polman, Unilever's current CEO, acted in the image of his company's founder when he created their Global Sustainable Living Plan. Unilever's current purpose is 'to make sustainable living commonplace'. They 'work to create a better future every day, with brands and services that help people feel good, look good, and get more out of life'.

They have defied the notion that growth is incompatible with sustainability by pledging to double their revenue whilst reducing their environmental footprint and increasing social impact.

This latest Polman-led era builds on the core purpose of their high-growth years in the twentieth century: 'To make cleanliness commonplace; to lessen work for women; to foster health.' Whilst tripartite in its claims, it has clear societal aims for which employees and partners worked hard and with pride.

Business undertakes many different approaches to social activity, but which pays back best to the business?

Keen to find out, Nancy Lee and Philip Kotler, marketing gurus, set out to study and segment different types of social activity pursued by brands and businesses.

They identified five different types. One type paid back to the business much more powerfully than the others. They identified this as 'corporate social marketing', meaning the brand pursued a social issue directly related to its business and then put it at the heart of the marketing plan.

Some of the world's most successful companies have organised themselves around the most important societal benefit of their *specific* products and services.

IKEA want to 'create a better everyday life for the many' via 'a wide range of well-designed, functional home furnishing at prices so low that as many people as possible will be able to afford them'.

Google have a mission 'to organise the world's information and make it universally accessible and useful'.

Toyota don't simply design cars but 'will lead the way to the future of mobility, enriching lives with the safest and most responsible ways of moving people'. This is a 100-year purpose.

Southwest Airlines don't just fly planes; they 'connect

people to what's important in their lives through friendly, reliable and low-cost air travel'. They recruit their staff on the basis of their sense of humour and their genuine rather than sickly pretend people skills. They have consistently been the highest-rated airline in America.

It is tangible, everyday behaviours that deliver the true value of a core purpose. These signature actions and behaviours make these core purposes successful decade after decade.

ICI for many years pursued a core purpose of 'the responsible application of chemistry' well before CSR became fashionable.

From its formation in 1928 until well into the 1980s, it was the largest manufacturer in Britain and a world leader in very diverse fields. It developed the plastic Perspex, Dulux paints, Terylene and Crimplene fibres and fabrics, and leading pharmaceuticals such as Paludrine and Tamoxifen, all under this common purpose.

Some brands have a great positioning but they only look at it through a business lens. Sometimes looking at your business purpose from a new angle can reveal a big opportunity that's totally true to the business whilst helping the world at large.

Years ago, I co-founded a consultancy called Circus. We set it up to strengthen brands from the inside out, rather than the usual route adopted by agencies of propping them up with clever, externally focused, communications campaigns.

We were appointed by NCR to rethink their purpose. In 1997, NCR had been spat out of the giant AT&T

telecommunications group and forced to make their own way in the world again (they had started life as National Cash Register, founded in 1884).

NCR are the global leaders in cash machines, self-service kiosks and other transactions equipment such as barcode scanners. They thought they wanted to get out of the oily rag world of machines – 'all this electro-mechanical equipment' – and go into the pure, clean and high-margin world of consultancy. We persuaded them not to.

We pointed out that a cash machine, if used properly, could be a device for developing relationships. For example, the bank's database knows if you often take money out from cash machines abroad and can offer you travel insurance. It knows you always take out £200 and so can save you time by offering 'Your usual £200'.

We thus persuaded them to stick by their excellence at transaction devices but ally this to an important cause by working to the mission of 'turning transactions into relationships'. It was an immediate and sustained success. One of the opportunities we pointed out was that banks could use cash machines to ask you to support local charities or vote on local issues. More than fifteen years after we first suggested it, banks are finally starting to use them as relationship devices and devices for good.

Core purpose, when done properly, emerges from the essence of a company, generating heat and light from the inside outwards. It expresses and strengthens a business's strategy. It is totally bespoke to that business and central to its future. It is like the nuclear fusion at the core of the sun that constantly emanates outwards.

Core purpose maximises all a company's or organisation's resources whether human or material and there is a growing body of evidence that companies who bring commercial and social purpose together in one clear core purpose outperform all their peers.

Why? Because employees don't leap out of bed in the morning to deliver quarterly profits for distant, institutional shareholders; they are motivated by a company that behaves like a miniature society in and of itself and which delivers something tangible and defined to society at large.

Companies that consistently manage and measure their responsible business activities outperformed their FTSE 350 peers on total shareholder return in seven of the last eight years according to data from the FTSE.

A Harvard Business School study in 2012 showed that the annual market performance of companies that are pursuing sustainability is 4.8 per cent higher than those who are not.

Those companies that have a well-communicated core purpose have up to a 17 per cent better financial performance according to an IMD/Burson Marsteller study in 2010/11.

Studies by Work USA in 2008/09, in 7,939 business units across thirty-six companies, found a clear connection between the profit-producing business outcomes of customer satisfaction, productivity, employee turnover, and reduced health costs and employee engagement.

Indeed, companies with employees who are genuinely

engaged experience 26 per cent higher revenue per colleague, 13 per cent higher total returns to shareholders, and a 50 per cent higher market premium.

The best prediction of a company or organisation's future value is more likely to come from studying employee motivation more than any other factor. This is entirely logical, as employees are exposed to a company or organisation for the majority of their waking hours. They have a much richer, more rounded and realistic view of a company than a consumer, investment analyst or opinion-former, all of whom are exposed to them a few hours a year.

Just think how transformational it would be if there were a widely adopted and agreed method for assessing both the robustness and stability and the future growth potential of companies by methodically measuring their employee engagement, retention and motivation.

Such an assessment is likely to be more informed by the complex realities of that business as understood by its employees, ergo more thorough as a form of investment analysis. It would encourage companies and their boards to genuinely treat their employees as their most important stakeholders, rather than just the ludicrous lip-service of saying, 'Our greatest assets go up and down in the lift every day.' This new focus would then produce happier employees, more productive employees and stronger companies. It would also encourage the mid-to-long-termism that is so famously lacking from the stock market.

I want to say a few final words about the basic societal commitments and good practice of businesses. Whilst it has been said many times, it doesn't seem to get enforced by consistent public lobbying and political willpower: we need all companies to pay their proper taxes.

The Tax Justice Network estimated in 2011 that the UK lost £69.9 billion a year in tax evasion and avoidance, pointing out that this was the equivalent of 56 per cent of the country's total healthcare spend.

More recently, Tax Research LLP calculated that the 'tax gap' between what should have been collected and what actually was collected was a staggering £119 billion in 2013/14. Even tackling half of this would go a long way towards cutting the deficit. The government of course disputes this and claims a much lower figure of £35 billion. Yet even that would make a substantial difference.

In 2013, Oxfam calculated that, even if the UK were only losing £5.2 billion a year in tax evasion, that equals nearly £200 per household, or £21 a week to every household experiencing fuel poverty, or the cost of doubling universal childcare entitlement to twenty-five hours a week.

That figure of £5.2 billion is close to the tax gap for businesses operating in Britain, estimated by the HMRC in 2013 at £4.7 billion. This figure excluded the controversial 'profit-shifting' schemes run by companies such as Google, Amazon and Starbucks, which would add another several billion and which the HMRC don't even recognise as being owed.

Some multinational businesses in the UK pay as little as 0.1 per cent tax. A *Sunday Mirror* analysis in 2013 showed that avoidance of corporation tax costs every British taxpayer £183 a year. That may be small beer for the rich but it's a flagon for the poor. Thirty per cent of it comes from just eight multinational companies and so it's not exactly difficult to enforce.

'Tax evasion is morally repugnant ... it's stealing from law-abiding people, who face higher taxes to make good the lost revenue.' So said not a left-wing anti-capitalist but George Osborne in August 2011 after a showdown with Swiss banks. You may have done something, George, but you need to do a lot more and that starts with employing more people at HMRC rather than cutting jobs. Employing more HMRC staff to clamp down on fraud would, to use a classic economist's phrase, represent one of the highest 'returns on investment' this country has ever seen.

In addition to paying their taxes, business CEOs should take note of the Gini co-efficient, the most commonly used measure of inequality of entire nations, within their own domains. Analysis by the High Pay think tank shows that the average CEO-to-worker pay ratio is currently 130:1 in the FTSE 100. To be absolutely explicit, this means that a CEO in those companies is being paid 130 times more per year than the average pay of those they lead.

In 1980, the ratio was between thirteen and forty-four, and in 1998 it was forty-seven. Research just published by Chulalongkorn University's Sorapop Kiatpongsan and Harvard Business School's Michael Norton shows the damaging difference between the ideal ratios for CEO pay that people across many countries think is fair and the actual ratios. The ideal pay ratio, averaged out across the forty countries, was

4.6:1 and the estimate of the reality was 10:1. In the UK, the actual ratio was 84. In France it's 104, in Germany 147 and in the US 354!

This disparity between the ideal ratio, or even a pragmatic compromise, and the actuality, explains the levels of demotivation now felt by employees across the developed world.

Levels of inequality are at their highest since the 1930s. As someone pointed out, in medieval society people knew they couldn't fight inequality. If they were born poor, they died poor.

Now people are constantly being told they can move upwards and then discovering, even the middle class, that there is a low glass ceiling crushing their spine, on which walk the feet of the super-rich. Business CEOs, take a lead! You can live the most fulfilling life possible on a fraction of your wages. Create a true legacy.

Chapter 13

Volunteering isn't worthy and charities are not the Third Sector

THE SUMMER OF 2012 was glorious for London, especially by contrast with the riots of the preceding summer. The world's eyes were on London for the Olympics and London gleamed in the spotlight. So much so that the aftermath has seen record numbers of tourists flock to the UK.

A key part of the success of the 2012 Olympics were the 70,000 volunteers or 'Games Makers', a clever piece of nomenclature that defined both their goal and importance. They were warm, funny, enthusiastic and well trained. According to many, they were the new face of volunteering and would inspire a fresh take on giving time.

This has sadly proved to be wrong, as levels of volunteering appear to have remained roughly constant, or even slightly declined, since 2012. It was always going to be wrong, because dressing up in a distinctive uniform, high-fiving crowds of excited visitors in largely great weather, getting free seats at spectacular events and occasionally meeting famous athletes is pretty uplifting but nothing like normal volunteering. It's much more rewarding on the surface but in many ways less transformational and meaningful for the volunteers concerned.

Yes, 70,000 people did a great job. Yes, they volunteered for a minimum of ten days with no pay, expenses or accommodation. Yet no one at the time chose to point out that every month of every year, not just one month, eleven to twelve million people – a quarter of the adult population – do some form of regular, formal volunteering. Many more volunteer informally. It is this regular army of time-givers who are the 'Community Makers', who don't get a uniform or high-fives or their picture in the newspaper, and they are the invisible utility that enables our society to function.

Business and public sector employers alike need to transform their view of volunteering in working hours beyond the polite tolerance and mild support that prevails. This need is based on the fact that the state can no longer provide all the support services that an ageing and growing population demands and we therefore need to think of volunteering as a kind of vital public utility like the health service. It's also because volunteering provides benefits to the individual and the employer alike.

Studies have shown that employee volunteering drives down absenteeism. It creates shared value systems helpful in the workplace (which is more meaningful than the rather vague notion of 'team building'). It also creates gratitude towards the employer, an increased allegiance. Indeed, neuroimaging has shown that volunteering releases dopamine in the brain, making us feel physically good.

We can argue about whether there is any such thing as 'pure altruism' or whether altruism plays a Darwinian role: the more an individual in a species helps others, the greater chance those others will then help them, in turn, to survive. Whatever the root motives, and they probably cover a spectrum from instant and pure sympathy to refined selfishness or pragmatism, the effect is undeniable and can be proven factually.

A large CVS study in 2013 showed that the costs of employee time away from work are outweighed by the business benefits, such as increased employee morale, loyalty and productivity. We all know from our own experience that breaking routine to do something different, challenging and absorbing enables us to return to our normal tasks with more energy, ingenuity and productivity. Yes, this can be playing sport, watching a play or reading a book, but it can also be volunteering. Why can't we apply this known truth at scale to volunteering?

I have mentioned that when we launched TimeBank, we used the concept of 'reverse mentoring': trying to capture the truth that the mentor gains as much as the mentee. TimeBank have many case histories of this proving to be true.

One retailer with a mature volunteering programme and 9,500 employees, working with TimeBank, achieved an annual saving of nearly £2 million through the motivational benefits of volunteering. It came to light when they compared staff turnover rates and found a dramatic decrease – from an average 19 per cent to 2.7 per cent – amongst those staff who took part in their employee volunteering programme.

One of the most revealing experiences in my work with charities has been with Pilotlight. Pilotlight operates what many might consider to be a curious system. People called Pilotlighters, many of them senior people from the professions, pay Pilotlight to match their skills and time with the needs of small charities. These smaller charities are vetted very carefully and are typically at a stage where, if they professionalised, they could grow and do more good.

In many ways, the typical path of a social entrepreneur is the same as that of their commercial counterparts. They start their organisation out of a passion and set of skills, and to get away from the politics, admin and bureaucracy of bigger organisations. They then quickly find that they are drowning in admin and cash-flow issues and need help to create a more mature organisational structure. This is what Pilotlighters do, spending twelve months mentoring charities, with a project manager overseeing the process.

Since 2003, they have recruited more than 1,000 business leaders to serve as mentors and coaches for over 400 charitable organisations, which work to help improve the lives of more than 3.6 million people, from children with learning disabilities to isolated older people.

The skills coaching they have provided to date is worth £11 million. On average, up to 2012, partner charities experience an increase in income of at least 50 per cent after their year of working with Pilotlight and are able to help almost twice as many people.

The achievements are impressive and what is very telling and moving is the reverse mentoring effect I have described. The charities are somewhat in awe of these very talented, confident, highly paid people whose service they are getting for free. Equally, the Pilotlighters themselves – many from the City of London – are humbled by how much charity leaders have achieved on very scant resources.

We really need Pilotlight on a huge scale. What they have revealed is a truth that so many people overlook: that the best kind of volunteering comes from your practical skills, passions, hobbies and life experiences. So many people volunteer because they feel they ought to. They can often then volunteer to do something they are not very good at, have a bad experience and then don't come back to volunteering for years, if ever.

It sounds like the most basic common sense, but not everyone has the patience or empathy to visit an elderly person or help with the disabled. Yet they may be brilliant at football and, through coaching, help youngsters with low self-esteem feel better about themselves.

This is why at Your Square Mile, we created a personal planner which asks you ten questions about your skills, hobbies, passions and life experiences. It then makes bespoke suggestions based on your answers. If organisations are serious about encouraging more volunteering amongst their colleagues then they need to use tools like this, as well as adopting a new mentality.

It rarely occurs to people that if they have experienced and survived bullying, redundancy, divorce, rape, domestic violence, cancer or simply being lonely, their experience can be the passport to other people learning how to survive it as well. The people who best solve social problems are, time and again, the people who have been their victims.

This one-to-one help can be done face-to-face or on the phone with organisations such as the Samaritans, ChildLine or The Silver Line, or even on the internet with organisations such as Horsesmouth. As the latter says, 'Someone knows what you need. Someone needs what you know.'

Some of the greatest needs that charities have, especially smaller charities, is for help in writing grant applications; doing their accounts; creating a business plan; finding and managing an office; complying with regulations. Even one hour a week of this kind of help is transformational and thank goodness that companies such as Barclays are starting to institutionalise this sharing of skills.

Small charities are the majority of charities. According to NCVO, in 2011/12, there were 82,391 charities earning less than £10,000 per year. They represented 51.1 per cent of all charities but only received 0.6 per cent of the sector's income. A further 52,815 charities had incomes of £10,000 to £100,000: 32.8 per cent of charities, who receive only 4.7 per cent of the sector's income.

Thus, more than eight out of ten charities are small or tiny and receive only one-twentieth of all charity income. By contrast, the top 533 charities get just under half the sector's income.

There are also estimated to be another 600,000 civic society organisations that are too small in terms of income to register with the Charity Commission. Many of them are not even registered with their local authority. This is what you might term the 'invisible or white economy' who do invaluable community work.

Smaller charities and civic society organisations tackle some of the toughest social problems in the UK but receive far less in terms of government or other support. They need the active help of local businesses and public sector organisations to survive or grow, and a small amount of time, skill or money makes an enormous difference.

Charities and social enterprises are grossly under-recognised by government and business alike. They are still seen by many, in a rather lame and Victorian way, as 'amateur do-gooders', nurses who patch up the bodies wounded by raw capitalism. Nothing could be further from the truth. Perhaps this is why they have been labelled the 'Third Sector', as if it were a ranking beneath the public and private sectors.

Charities and social enterprises develop new and unique problem-solving ideas often on modest resources. They are developers and owners of strong intellectual capital with a tangible value.

Andy Haldane, chief economist of the Bank of England, has commented on this recently in the Pro Bono Economics lecture. He points out that there is only one FTSE board member from a charity background, despite their enormous experience and value. He states: 'Charity chief executives often preside over huge budgets, have to motivate people willing to work for nothing or very little, manage services all over the country or abroad, and have to build and protect their brand.'

The ONS 2012/13 figures for the value of just those people who volunteer monthly, let alone those who volunteer less frequently, is 2.1 billion hours and a monetary value of £23.9 billion. Haldane goes on to estimate that all UK volunteering might total 4.4 billion hours per year, nearly 10 per cent of the total hours of the paid workforce, with a value of £50 billion or 3.5 per cent of GDP.

Of course, that is just the value of the volunteering time, without considering the value of the problem-solving services delivered by not-for-profits in saving government and society money. It is also just volunteering at its current level, in which roughly a quarter of adults volunteer on a monthly or more frequent basis. Imagine how much greater it could be.

According to Global Enterprise Monitor, in 2007 there were 238,000 social entrepreneurs in the UK. They are much more ethnically diverse than the population at large, perhaps reflecting the tougher challenges minorities often face. They are also gender-balanced compared to the more male-oriented world of commercial start-ups, reflecting the fact that women are often better at social action.

Many social entrepreneurs come from tough backgrounds themselves. Only 1 per cent of them get any kind of formal funding. Imagine if they were given the same opportunities and access to funding as their commercial counterparts.

One of the worst failings of the Big Society was that charities were promised a crack at delivering public services in exchange for diminished government funding but in the end they were all given to companies such as Serco. The measurement and payment-by-results framework was totally alien to charities, for a start.

There was much talk of people giving less to charity in the recession. In the net result, whilst there was a small dip from 2007 to 2009, from 2010 to 2012 a higher proportion of people gave to charity: 58 per cent. This still means that four out of ten people do not give to charity in the course of the year. We need to work hard to change that situation by educating and inspiring people about the quantifiable difference charities make to the society they are living in.

In 2009/10, individuals contributed £14.3 billion to charity and by 2011/12 it had increased to £17.4 billion. By contrast, government funding dropped from £13.9 billion to £13.7 billion. The private sector gave £1.8 billion.

In other words, individuals give far more money than government and are increasing what they give. Government only provides one-third of voluntary sector funding and it's reducing. Individuals give ten times as much as businesses.

It's about time that politicians and businesses respected the intellectual capital, ingenuity and value for money that the sector they derogatorily put in third place, behind them, delivers. We need charities to be given far fairer means of tendering for public service provision.

We need government to see upholding the level of financial support for UK-based charities in real, inflation-adjusted terms as sacrosanct as the foreign aid budget.

We need wider support for ideas such as social impact bonds. We need the financial service providers to create social impact ISAs and bonds so that ordinary citizens with savings can invest in charities and social entrepreneurs who serve a particular cause or neighbourhood they are passionate about.

Just as left and right in politics, or the 'LibLabCon' as it's sometimes called, has to be replaced by new dimensions and greater consensus, collaboration and real democracy, so the divisions between public, private and voluntary sectors in terms of thinking and stereotyping also need to change. Problem-solving capability, the drive for good value and many other things are shared across all three sectors. They have more to learn from, and give to, each other than anyone has yet recognised.

Look at the doubling of capacity that Pilotlight achieves with smaller charities in a short period of time. If the Tories had formed an intelligent, structured approach with the voluntary sector, then the Big Society might have started to become a reality.

Whenever I get depressed about the seemingly intractable problems we face, I think of the years of ingenuity I have seen from the voluntary sector. I think of the Peto Institute, started by Dr Andras Peto in 1945. It teaches children who have cerebral palsy and cannot control their bodies properly to lead more independent lives by means of conductive education; they retrain the muscles and neural pathways.

I think of the Chicken Shed Theatre putting children with behavioural problems in charge of children with disabilities and thereby raising their self-esteem and skills through trust. I also think of the Shakespeare Schools Festival, which encourages children of all backgrounds to do Shakespeare in a lively, unstuffy way and confounds any views that the most complex language cannot be made discernible to all. The most captivating Lady Macbeth I have ever seen was by a young black teenager from a tough state school in this festival.

I think about the car park owner in Lagos, Nigeria, who, worn out by the constant stealing and vandalising of cars in his charge, rounded up the villains and made them his security force, with huge success.

I think about St Giles Trust, and similar organisations,

having an ex-offender waiting there at the prison gates at 4 p.m. on a Friday when a prisoner is released and helping them get through the first critical weeks when they are so tempted to re-offend.

I think of Bill Lawns travelling ninety minutes each way every day to run the centre in Pollokshields, Glasgow, that brings warmth and stimulation to a poor neighbourhood, who says he has the best job in the world; and the tens of thousands of people like him.

I think of Trevor Baylis's wind-up radio that has allowed anyone in the remotest area, with no electricity, to have the comfort of the human voice.

I think of the many people who have survived drug abuse and domestic violence and crushing poverty and children being killed who dedicate themselves to stop it happening to other people or to help those who also fall victim.

These are the reasons to be cheerful, to believe in the true strength of the human species: empathy, ingenuity and determination.

I would like these people to come to the fore, to be their own politicians, which is the subject of my last chapter.

Chapter 14

The People's Parliament

BETWEEN 15 AND 19 June 1215, in a peaceful water meadow near Windsor called Runnymede, a document was fashioned and agreed that was variously a peace agreement, a charter and a legal document, called Magna Carta. It is sometimes known as the Great Charter of the Liberties of England and it changed the course of world history. This year we celebrate its 800th anniversary.

There are many myths about Magna Carta. King John never

signed it. Rather, he sealed it in green-dyed beeswax the size of a fist. It didn't contain habeas corpus, nor create the first parliament, but it did contain the principles that led to both.

It contained sixty-three clauses, many of which were very particular and related to practical issues of the day such as fish-weirs in the Thames impeding the ships of the London merchants. 'Arbitrary treatment' by the King was Magna Carta's unifying enemy across these clauses.

One of the most interesting aspects of the charter, revealed in the excellent recent programmes by the BBC, was that it was protean in nature. Written in condensed, medieval Latin on sheepskins, with many technical terms, it has always been, rather like Biblical texts, open to many different translations and interpretations at different ages, for different generations. This has been a great strength.

Its fundamental ideas and principles are immensely powerful. The Fifth Amendment from the American Bill of Rights – the right to a fair trial – is one of the most important examples.

It is the document that led to the rule of constitutional law in England and beyond. Whilst it was negotiated by the feudal barons, it contained rights that were vital to all citizens, including an agreement that taxes should only be levied by the 'common counsel of the realm', which became Parliament.

It thus lays down fundamental human and citizen rights. It also granted freedom to the English Church. It established the beginnings of local government and democracy by demanding that twelve knights should be elected in every county by the county court. This was a very narrow democracy but a lot wider than a single king.

The concept of an actual parliament came later and grew out of the Curia Regis: a council or court that included prominent church leaders and the land-owning aristocracy and which advised the king. The term 'parliamentum' was used in the general sense of a meeting at which negotiations took place and it was first officially used for the meetings of the Court of the King's Bench in 1236, twenty-one years after the original Magna Carta.

In 1265, Simon de Montfort's parliament was the first parliament to have representatives that were elected not appointed, and to include non-peers/commoners in the form of two burgesses or aldermen elected from every borough. It was the forerunner of the House of Commons.

It met from 20 January to 15 February 1265, 750 years ago, and took place in the original, not current, Westminster Hall and also in the Chapter House at Westminster Abbey.

The Chapter House, a beautiful octagonal building, was also used repeatedly for the King's Great Council from 1257 and for the House of Commons in the late fourteenth century. It is thus the perfect place to revisit the role of the people in Parliament as well as the role of the Church and other religions in engaging with and helping to solve societal problems.

That is precisely what a group of us want to do. We are planning to create a People's Parliament, to be held in the same venue as de Montfort's parliament in Westminster Abbey: a parliament that goes back to the roots of democracy, to the principles of Magna Carta and makes them contemporary.

We hope the BBC will be our partners and we already have the enthusiastic and thoughtful encouragement of John Hall, the Dean of Westminster Abbey, and his Chapter.

Religious principles form the basis of our morality and our code of law. Religious venues have a history of being used as marketplaces, thoroughfares, debating chambers and performance spaces as well as places for prayer and sanctuary. We want to build on that and restore that role.

Many of our toughest social problems are solved or helped by religious practices that could find wider adoption in society and they are very topical.

For example, the way we solve food poverty can be helped by understanding the provision of the 'Langar' free community meals in the Sikh Gurdwara or Christian soup kitchens.

On the growing problem of crippling debt and pay-day loan sharks, we can learn from the Islamic ban on charging interest or from the Christian principles surrounding money-lending.

We therefore want to bring faith-based approaches, amongst others, to the creation of a genuinely democratic and problem-solving People's Parliament.

Our idea is to re-engage the disengaged and give a voice to the poor, the disenfranchised and to the inspiring but largely invisible change agents in our society.

We will determine the ten most pressing problems facing society via a comprehensive survey of a representative cross-section of the British public. The ideas are likely to include topics such as care for the elderly, loneliness, food poverty, youth unemployment, homelessness, immigration, the NHS and re-offending.

We will then invite people to step forward who are already implementing inspiring and practical solutions to those ten problems. People can either step forward themselves or nominate someone else.

We want to find people who are the 'unheard voices' and problem-solvers of the UK on those topics, including: social entrepreneurs; charity leaders; train, taxi and bus drivers; air traffic controllers; hospital porters; nurses; cleaners; factory workers; engineers; police on the beat; lollipop ladies; border control staff; social workers; carers; teachers; independent experts who have strong, tangible ideas; and people from a wide variety of faiths.

From that pool of problem-solvers, 650 change agents will be elected to mirror the 650 MPs voted into Parliament in the general election.

We would like to make a short film to showcase every one of our 650 selected doers and their solutions. The 650 filmed ideas would then be put online, searchable by topic, and will develop followers and communities via social media.

We would then want to conduct a well-publicised vote in which the public selects the ten best ideas. We hope these ideas would be vividly presented by their advocates, using all the power of good storytelling, at a special televised and web-streamed event to take place at the Chapter House in Westminster Abbey.

We would then follow the progress of the ten ideas and

their People's Parliament advocates, and press for Parliament to adopt them.

This isn't a substitute for reforming mainstream politics but we hope it could be a vital catalyst and give people the power to express their best ideas, to be heard.

Conclusion:
the really big picture

NOW, MORE THAN EVER, we need the perspective of the twenty-four astronauts who have escaped our earth orbit and seen our planet from the moon: fragile, perched at exactly the right distance from the sun to sustain life.

Over the past 150 years, the world's industrialised nations have unwittingly upset the delicate balance of the carbon cycle by burning huge amounts of fossil fuels ('stored, ancient sunlight' in the form of coal, oil, gas), as well as breeding vast numbers of methane-producing livestock, and cutting down the forests that naturally absorb CO_2 from the air.

We know the planet has warmed by an average of nearly 1°C in the past century. 2°C is too much and will mean severe storms and floods in some countries, droughts in many more. Seas will become more acidic, coral and krill will die, food chains will be destroyed. There will be no Arctic ice in summer, which means the global climate will warm even faster.

Scientists predict possible rises of up to 6°C this century if we don't drastically cut greenhouse gas emissions. This would mean rainforests dying, the melting of the ancient ice sheets of Greenland and Antarctica, and dramatic sea-level rises.

We need to cut greenhouse gas emissions by at least 40 per cent from 1990 levels by 2020, and at least 80 per cent by 2050.

The world's wildlife population is half the size it was in the 1970s according to WWF's Living Planet Report. Yes, that is half. BBC Radio 4's *Today* programme recently played the sounds of a rainforest habitat decades ago and now. The near silence of now said more than a thousand statistics. It is the sound of Eden, our Mother Earth, dying.

To quote David Nussbaum, CEO of WWF UK: 'Humans are cutting down trees more quickly than they can regrow, overfishing the world's oceans, pumping rivers and aquifers dry and emitting more carbon than can be absorbed.' When in God's name will we wake up? When will we stop this brutal rape?

Those most affected by global warming will be the poor, to add to their existing woes. Nearly half the world's population – over three billion people – lives on less than $2.50 a day. Approximately 1.1 billion people have inadequate access to water; 1.6 billion live without electricity and 2.6 billion people lack basic sanitation.

Over nine million people die each year because of hunger and malnutrition. Five million of them are children. Up to 30,000 children a day die of poverty: that's a child every three seconds. There were estimated to be 925 million hungry people in 2010: one in seven people alive.

The poorest 40 per cent of the world's population accounts for 5 per cent of global income. The richest 20 per cent accounts for 75 per cent. These crushing problems don't just exist in less developed countries. Two million teenagers live on the streets in a country as wealthy as the US.

The average life expectancy of the richest 10 per cent in the UK is fourteen years longer than the poorest 10 per cent and they have 100 times more wealth. If travelling on the London Underground from Westminster to east London, every two Tube stops represents more than a year of life expectancy lost. Between Lancaster Gate and Mile End the average life expectancy decreases by twelve years.

Many have suffered from the average drop in income of £1,800 since 2010: those fighting against unfair cuts in benefits; the majority whose children cannot afford to buy a home; the large number who are on zero-hour contracts, not earning a living wage or unemployed; the growing number using food banks or who are either homeless or living in overcrowded housing.

So much poverty in UK is invisible. The Economic and Social Research Council found that 2.5 million children live in homes that are damp and 1.5 million in homes that can't afford heating; and that 5.5 million adults go without essential clothing. The stereotype is that these people are scroungers and yet many of them work; or that they have Sky TV subscriptions so aren't really poor. This ignores the fact that all your pleasures have to be in the home if you can't afford holidays or restaurants or the cinema.

Even if some people do find it difficult to prioritise their spending and could cut back on booze and fags, as so many would have you believe, the only way out of their problems is to have greater self-esteem, a broader range of helpful, non-judgemental people in their lives. Being branded as parasites on society will only make these things far less likely to happen.

If future generations exist, they will be truly aghast that we fiddled with party politics whilst the planet burned and poverty grew. What happened to the very green Mr Cameron? Why is Green a party and not a golden thread running through every party's manifesto or the framework for all their economic policies?

If the UK wants to be a global leader again, it can be a leader in making our lives more sustainable, our society and world more equal. This will require a wholly new kind of politics.

This new kind of politics needs to operate on a swift and fluid exchange of ideas and power from local to national to global and back again. It needs to harness digital technology to gather opinions and disseminate ideas on a frequent basis.

So government needs to work in ever-closer and more respectful partnership with charities and social enterprises on the one hand and businesses on the other.

Just as businesses get more engaged employees by having a clear and motivating core purpose that is about more than just profit, so societies work better and have more engaged citizens when a society's and its government's core purpose is about more than just economics.

We are all vulnerable and we are all capable and we all need to work together in that knowledge: all sixty-four million of us in the UK, all 7.3 billion of us on this planet.

Reproduced with permission of *Third Sector*

About the author

P AUL TWIVY'S CAREER HAS included working with the last three UK prime ministers on their big initiatives to develop a new partnership between citizens and government and to tackle ingrained social problems. He co-founded groundbreaking social action campaigns including TimeBank, Change the World for a Fiver, The Big Lunch, Big Society and Your Square Mile. Paul spent twenty-five years advising Comic Relief and is one of the best-known thinkers and innovators in British and global advertising. Paul is married with five children and lives in London.

271